AIRCRAFT ARCHIVE

POST-WAR JETS
VOLUME 2

Contents

A DETAILED COLLECTION OF ORIGINAL SCALE AIRCRAFT DRAWINGS

Introduction

In the first of these volumes we introduced the series of scale drawings with an explanation of their origins and importance as a permanent record of aircraft shapes, and credited the skills of the draughtsmen involved. This second volume extends the range of types which have been taken from the files of 'Aeromodeller' and 'Scale Models', two of the monthly magazines published by the original Model Aeronautical Press, long since absorbed into Argus Specialist Publications.

Although some of the drawings cover the earliest versions of types which were to be developed through many detail changes during long and varied service life, they illustrate the aircraft in its purest form and, for that reason alone, it is important that they perpetuate the first concept.

The clean lines of the first F-86 Sabre or the adventurous Leduc 021 belong to an era that will never return – before aircraft engineering became an assembly of compromise and outlines took on the image of committee decisions. Equally, the experiment of the F7U Cutlass, which proceeded to US Navy squadron service, or the bold, belly-landing Baroudeur, which was overtaken by the pace of progress, are each here to be compared in similar scale as representative of the spirit of challenge which was so evident in the 1950s. Not that such a spirit is dead and gone, for the Sea Harrier, which established itself in the Falklands, and the EAP test aircraft, itself a mix of components blended to prove potential for the future, are typical of the design innovation which aeronautical engineering generates.

In fact, out of the twenty-two aircraft types in this *Post-War Jets* volume, only one can be claimed to follow 'straight' convention, that being the jet variant of the Percival Provost trainer. It might be claimed that the diminutive Sparrowjet conversion from the Sparrowhawk racer was a similarly 'simple' modification: but for those who were fortunate enough to view its turbine installation and witness its flight, this admirable private venture is a more than justified inclusion among the unconventional.

So here we have quite a mixture – from swing-wings and VTOL to flying wings, twin booms and deltas. For the modeller, the student of aircraft shapes and the collector, this archive of *Post-War Jets* is a tribute to the manufacturers, and to the draughtsmen who pieced together the accurate outlines.

Each set of plans is a typical example of the skill and dedication applied by an amateur researcher over countless hours of translating measurements and interpreting photographs into a scale drawing which, in fact, no manufacturer could ever provide! For it may come as a

◄ '. . . The aircraft in its purest form . . .': the De Havilland DH110, prototype for the Royal Navy's Sea Vixen all-weather missile fighter.

'The clean lines of the first F-86 Sabre . . .'

surprise, but the reality is that the manufacturer's general arrangement drawings have little value in the factories, are rarely accurate in shape or scale and, without exception, illustrate the aeroplane in a stage long since superseded by production variants.

Access to the real thing is the ideal, but how can one measure each panel, check every angle and record all the shapes? It takes a special sort of dedication to undertake such a mammoth task – a museum visit will confirm the enormity of the undertaking.

Demand for accuracy and authenticity originated through the work of James Hay Stevens in 'Aeromodeller'. He was among the first to adopt 1/72nd scale, based on the Imperial measure of one sixth of an inch representing one foot. Opening standards, as set by James Stevens, were taken up through the series of *Aircraft of the Fighting Powers* volumes published by Harborough, once an associated company with MAP. Wartime urgency quickly generated a new breed of detail draughtsman, typified by Harry Cooper and Owen Thetford. After seven volumes and the creation of an *Aircraft Described* series, centred on civil aircraft by Eddie Riding, 1/72nd scale was firmly established, and the fine detail in the drawings reached levels of intricacy to satisfy the most demanding enthusiast – though not for long! Aeromodellers have an insatiable appetite for scale information.

From the immediate postwar years to the present day, the levels of minutiae have soared far beyond the first conceptions. Out of *Aircraft Described* came *Aeroplanes in Outline* and *Famous Biplanes*, and, through forty years of publication in 'Aeromodeller' magazine, a band of skilled contributors built up a series which now comes in book form.

The drawings reflect the individual character of the originator. Each was in its time a labour of love, the fruits of which have been the immense pleasure given to students, collectors and aeromodellers. If by reproduction in this form we commemorate their work permanently, rather than in a transient monthly magazine, then we will have rewarded both the draughtsmen and the reader with a treasure store.

Chance Vought F7U-3 Cutlass

Country of origin: USA.
Type: Single-seat, carrier-based fighter-bomber.
Dimensions: Wing span 39ft 8in *12.09m*; length 44ft 3in *13.49m*; height 14ft 7in *4.45m*; wing area 496 sq ft *46.08m²*.
Weights: Empty 15,600lb *7075kg*; maximum 31,650lb *14,353kg*.

Powerplant: Two Westinghouse J46-8B afterburning turbojets each of 6000lb *1829kg* maximum thrust.
Performance: Maximum speed 696mph *1120kph*; initial climb rate 17,500ft/min *5335m/min*; service ceiling 41,000ft *12,500m*; range (maximum external fuel) 1400 miles *2250km*.

Armament: Four fixed 20mm M2 cannon, plus (optional) up to 5500lb *2500kg* of external ordnance, including (-3M) four AAM-N-2 (Sparrow I) AAMs.
Service: First flight (XF7U-1) 29 September 1948, (F7U-1) 1 March 1950, (F7U-3) 20 December 1951; service entry (-3) 1953.

DRAWN BY J R ENOCH

Colour notes
Natural metal, with red in area uncovered by leading-edge slots when open; black windscreen frame, walkways, lettering, fin tops and nose cap; chrome yellow nose refuelling probe and crossed scimitars insignia on outside faces of fins; and brown jet pipes.

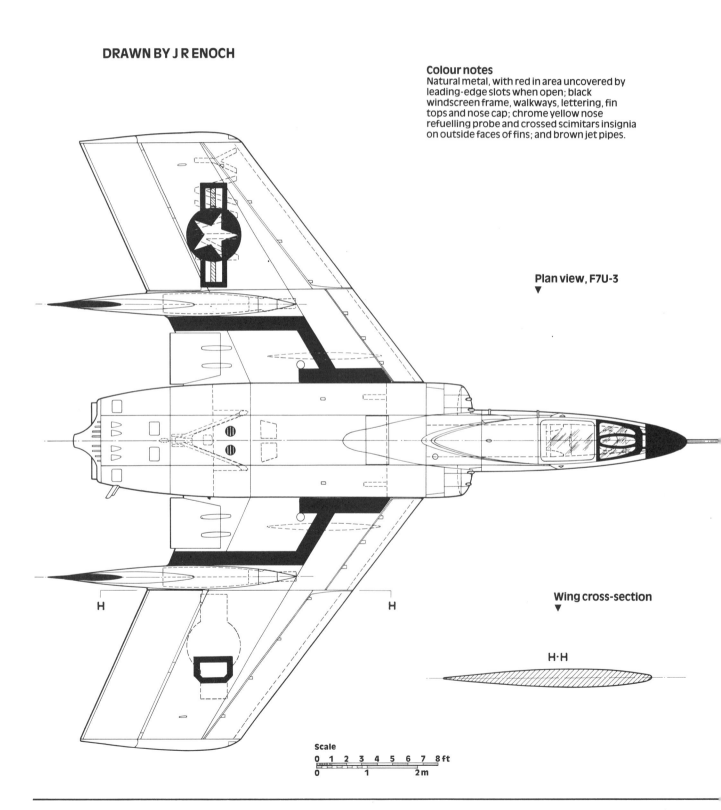

Plan view, F7U-3 ▼

Wing cross-section ▼

H·H

Scale
0 1 2 3 4 5 6 7 8ft
0 1 2m

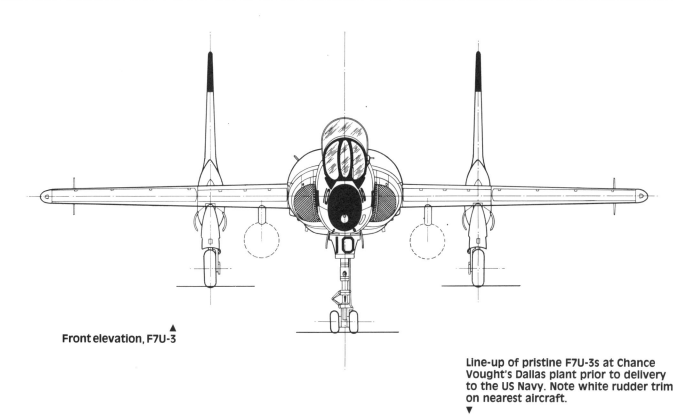

Front elevation, F7U-3

Line-up of pristine F7U-3s at Chance Vought's Dallas plant prior to delivery to the US Navy. Note white rudder trim on nearest aircraft.
▼

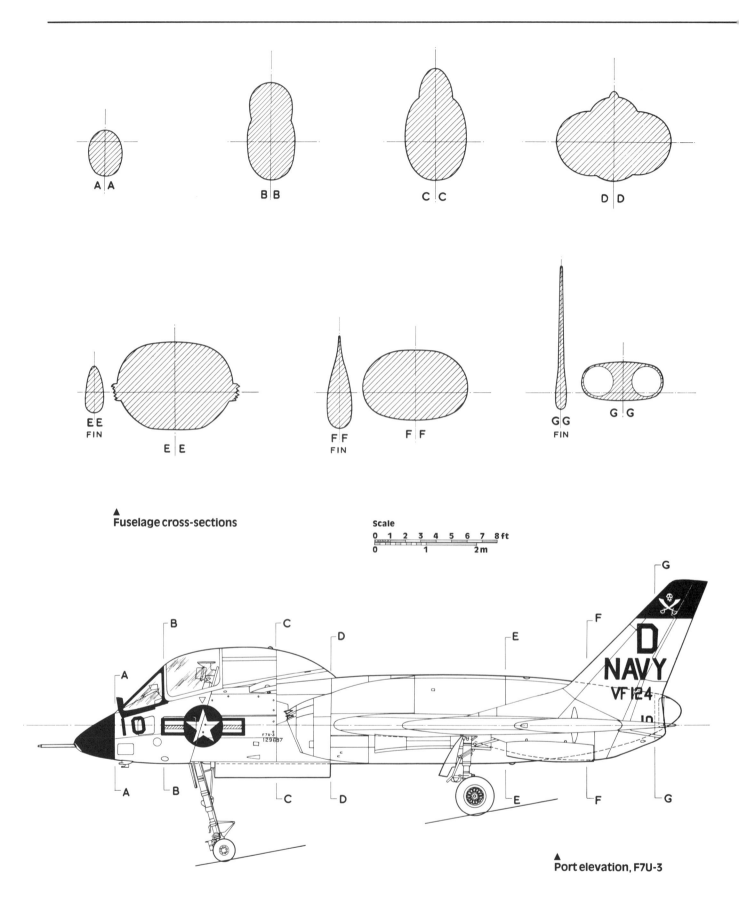

▲ Fuselage cross-sections

Scale

0 1 2 3 4 5 6 7 8 ft

0 1 2m

▲ Port elevation, F7U-3

'Ailevators' up, a VA-83 Cutlass lands aboard HMS *Eagle*, July 1956. Aircraft number appears above jet pipes as well as on forward fuselage.►▲

Missile-capable F7U-3M in later standard Navy scheme of Gull Gray and Insignia White. The Cutlass was notable in being the first fighter to feature afterburners.►▼

De Havilland DH110

Country of origin: Great Britain.
Type: Two-seat, carrier-based all-weather fighter prototype.
Dimensions: Wing span 50ft 0in *15.24m*; length 53ft 6in *16.31m*; height 11ft *3.35m*; wing area 648 sq ft *60.2m²*.

Weights: Loaded about 32,000lb *14,500kg*.
Powerplant: Two Rolls-Royce Avon turbojets each of about 7500lb *3400kg* static thrust.
Performance: Maximum speed about

650mph *1050kph*; initial climb rate 10,000ft/min *3050m/min*; service ceiling 48,000ft *14,630m*.
Armament: (Designed) Four fixed 30mm Aden cannon.
Service: First flight 26 September 1951.

DRAWN BY J R ENOCH

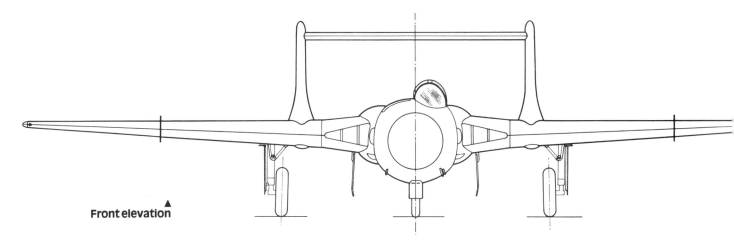

Front elevation ▲

▲
Second prototype DH110 WG240, which tragically disintegrated at the 1952 SBAC display at Farnborough.

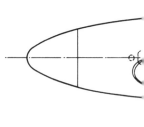

Port elevation
▼

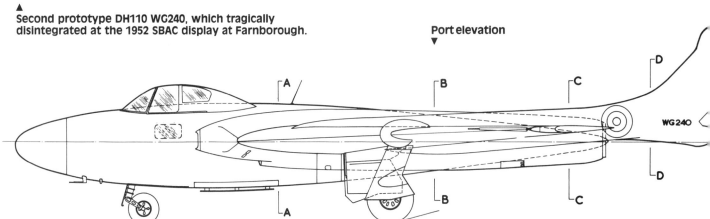

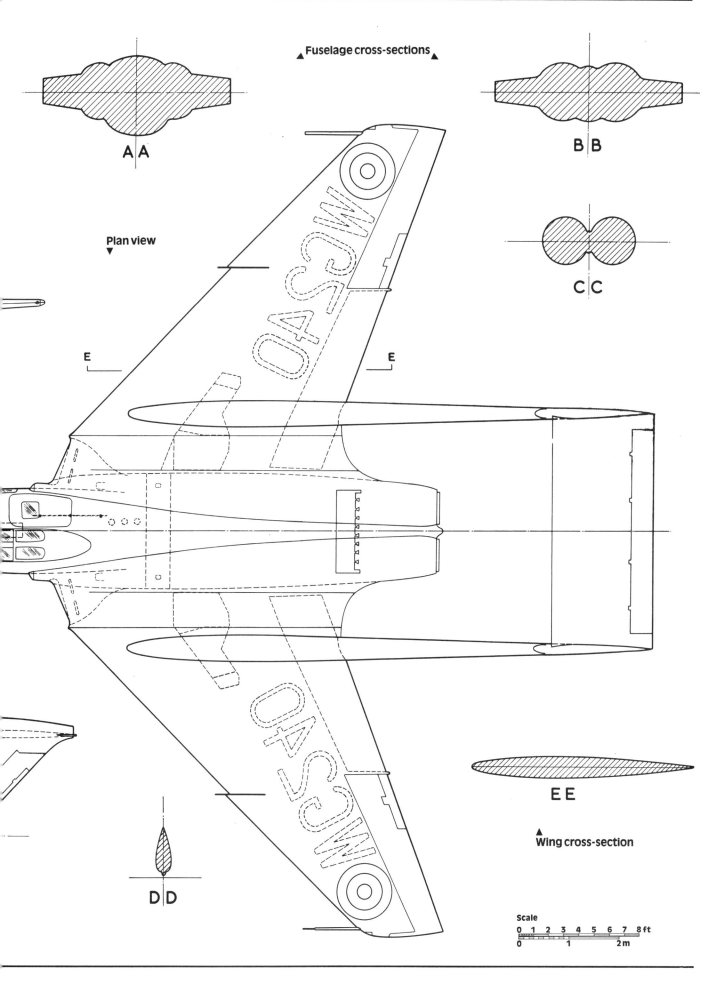

Fuselage cross-sections

A A

B B

C C

Plan view

E E

Wing cross-section

D D

Scale

0	1	2	3	4	5	6	7	8 ft

0	1	2 m

North American F-86E Sabre

Country of origin: USA.
Type: Single-seat, land-based fighter and fighter-bomber.
Dimensions: Wing span 37ft 1in *11.30m*; length 37ft 6in *11.45m*; height 14ft 0in *4.27m*; wing area 288 sq ft *26.76m²*.
Weights: Loaded 16,500lb *7483kg*.
Powerplant: One General Electric J47-GE-

13 axial-flow turbojet of 5200lb *2358kg* static thrust.
Performance: Maximum speed 670mph *1080kph*; initial climb rate 8000ft/min *2440m/min*; service ceiling 53,000ft *16,150m*; range (maximum external fuel) 2350 miles *3785km*.
Armament: Six fixed 0.5in machine guns,

plus (optional) sixteen 5in *127mm* rockets and up to 4000lb *1814kg* or bombs.
Service: First flight (XP-86) 1 October 1947; service entry (F-86A) December 1948, (E) early 1951.

Wing cross-section ▼

D D

Front elevation, F-86E ▶

Plan view, F-86E ▶

D

D

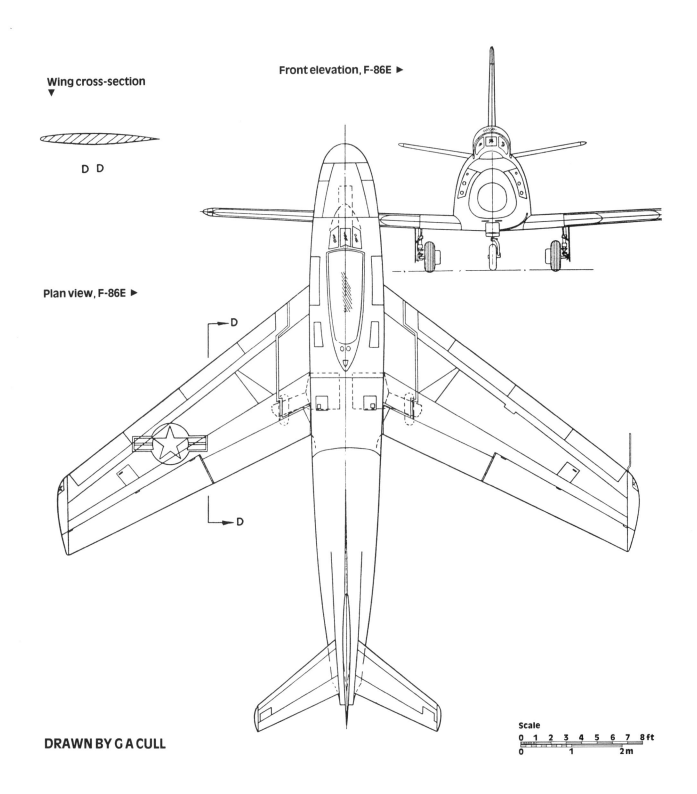

Scale
0 1 2 3 4 5 6 7 8 ft
0   1   2 m

DRAWN BY G A CULL

Port elevation, F-86E
▼

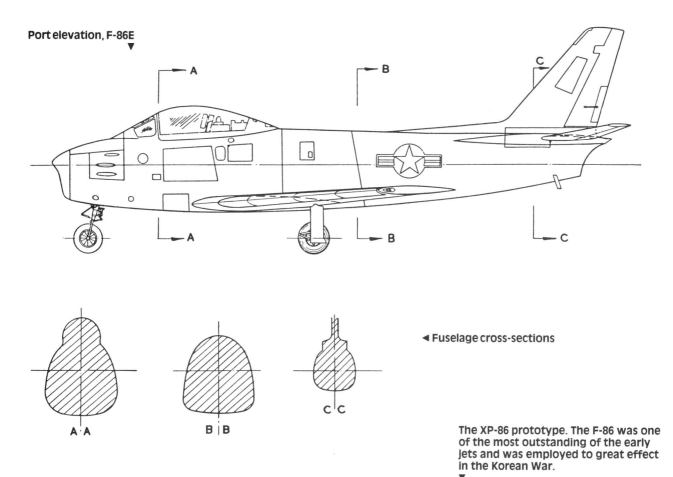

◄ **Fuselage cross-sections**

The XP-86 prototype. The F-86 was one of the most outstanding of the early jets and was employed to great effect in the Korean War.
▼

Hawker Hunter F Mk 5

Country of origin: Great Britain.
Type: Single-seat, land-based fighter.
Dimensions: Wing span 33ft 8in *10.26m*;
length 45ft 11in *14.00m*; height 13ft 2in
4.01m; wing area about 345 sq ft *32.00m²*.
Weights: Empty 12,543lb *5691kg*; loaded
17,100lb *7759kg*.

Powerplant: One Armstrong Siddeley
Sapphire 101 turbojet of 8000lb *3630kg*
thrust.
Performance: Maximum speed 720mph
1160kph (Mach 0.95) at sea level; initial
climb rate 8000ft/min *2440 m/min*;
service ceiling 50,000ft *15,240m*; range

about 480 miles *775km*.
Armament: Four fixed 30mm Aden
cannon.
Service: First flight (prototype) 20 July
1951, (Mk 5) 19 October 1954; service
entry (Mk 5) March 1955.

Port elevation, P.1067 prototype
▼

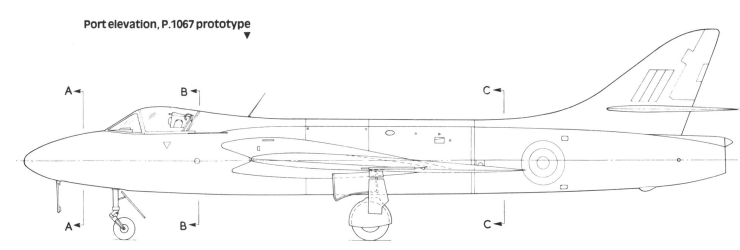

DRAWN BY G A G COX

The P.1067, first prototype Hunter, originally carried pale
green paintwork, as in these photos.
▼▶

Plan view, P.1067 prototype
▼

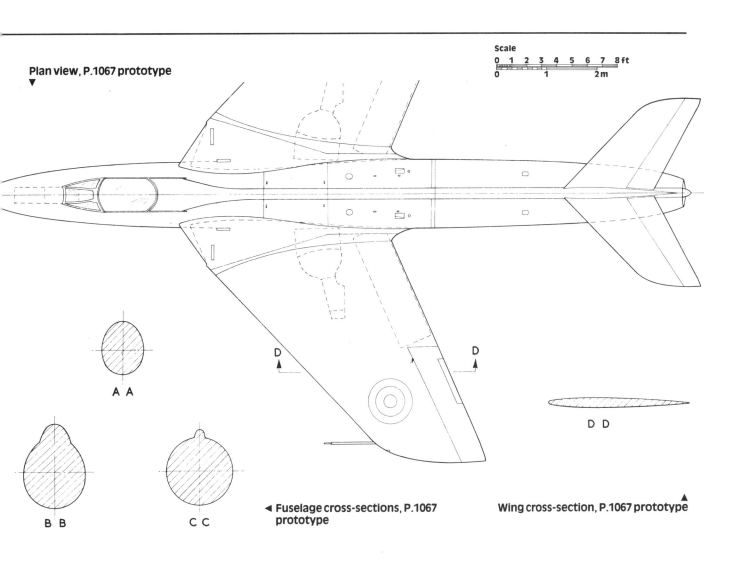

Scale
0 1 2 3 4 5 6 7 8 ft
0   1   2 m

A A

B B

C C

D D

◄ **Fuselage cross-sections, P.1067 prototype**

Wing cross-section, P.1067 prototype ▲

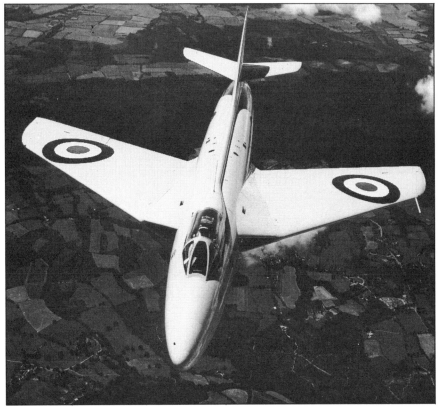

With an afterburner and twin speed brakes fitted, a new nose shape, red paintwork and a new designation – Hunter Mk 3 – the P.1067 achieved a new world air speed record of 727.6mph in September 1953.

Front elevation, P.1067 prototype
▼

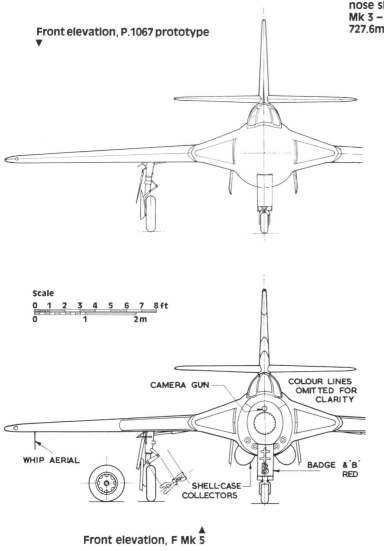

Scale

0 1 2 3 4 5 6 7 8 ft

0 1 2 m

WHIP AERIAL

CAMERA GUN

COLOUR LINES OMITTED FOR CLARITY

SHELL-CASE COLLECTORS

BADGE & 'B' RED

Front elevation, F Mk 5

SQUADRON LEADER'S RANK BADGE TOP TO BOTTOM DARK BLUE LIGHT BLUE, RED, LIGHT BLUE, DARK BLUE, BLACK EAGLE.

ALL RED EXCEPT WHITE LETTERING ON TRIANGLE

BLACK <u>OUTLINE</u> WHITE

RED

WHITE

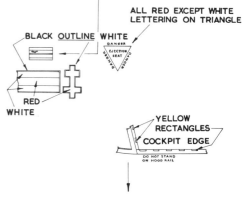

YELLOW RECTANGLES

COCKPIT EDGE

Port elevation, F Mk 5 ▶

NOSE-WHEEL TWICE FULL-SIZE

DESTRUCTOR

FOR INSCRIPTIONS

Colour notes, F Mk 5
Upper surfaces – Dark Green and Dark Sea
Grey; under surfaces – silver. All lettering
black unless otherwise stated.

▲
The Hunter first entered service thirty-five years ago, and
small numbers are still in use around the world. This shot
emphasises the aircraft's handsome lines.

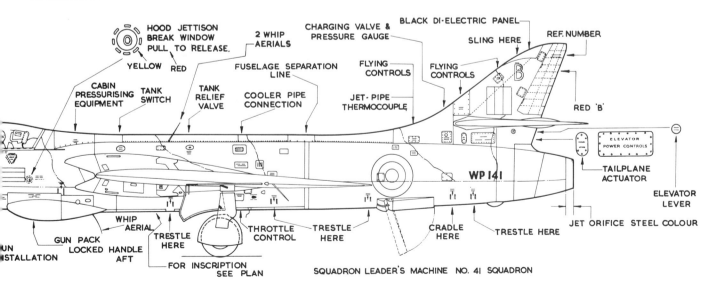

HOOD JETTISON
BREAK WINDOW
PULL TO RELEASE.

YELLOW   RED

2 WHIP
AERIALS

CHARGING VALVE &
PRESSURE GAUGE

BLACK DI-ELECTRIC PANEL

SLING HERE

REF. NUMBER

CABIN
PRESSURISING
EQUIPMENT

TANK
SWITCH

TANK
RELIEF
VALVE

FUSELAGE SEPARATION
LINE

COOLER PIPE
CONNECTION

FLYING
CONTROLS

FLYING
CONTROLS

FLYING
CONTROLS

JET-PIPE
THERMOCOUPLE

RED 'B'

ELEVATOR
POWER CONTROLS

WP 141

TAILPLANE
ACTUATOR

ELEVATOR
LEVER

JET ORIFICE STEEL COLOUR

GUN PACK
LOCKED HANDLE
AFT

WHIP
AERIAL

TRESTLE
HERE

THROTTLE
CONTROL

TRESTLE
HERE

CRADLE
HERE

TRESTLE HERE

FOR INSCRIPTION
SEE PLAN

GUN
INSTALLATION

SQUADRON LEADER'S MACHINE NO. 41 SQUADRON

◄ Hunter F.4s (RR Avon engine) soar vertically in a formation practice. One aircraft is from No 118 Squadron and the rest from No 93, RAF Germany.

▲
One of the Hunter's many export customers was Sweden, which purchased 120 Mk 50s (similar to Mk 4) from 1955. Many were modified to fire Sidewinder AAMs.

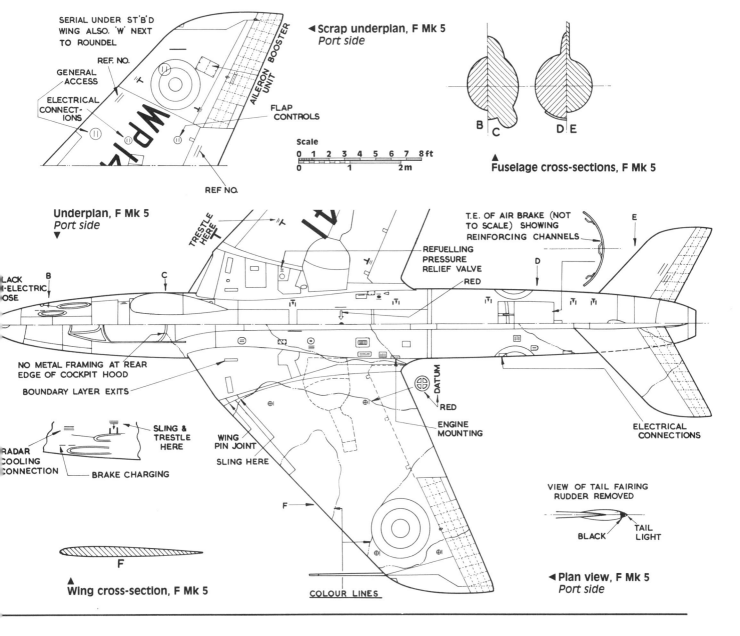

SERIAL UNDER ST'B'D WING ALSO. 'W' NEXT TO ROUNDEL

REF. NO.

GENERAL ACCESS

ELECTRICAL CONNECT-IONS

AILERON BOOSTER UNIT

FLAP CONTROLS

REF NO.

◄ Scrap underplan, F Mk 5
Port side

Scale
0 1 2 3 4 5 6 7 8 ft
0   1   2 m

B C   D E

▲ Fuselage cross-sections, F Mk 5

Underplan, F Mk 5
Port side
▼

TRESTLE HERE

T.E. OF AIR BRAKE (NOT TO SCALE) SHOWING REINFORCING CHANNELS

E

REFUELLING PRESSURE RELIEF VALVE

RED

D

BLACK ELECTRIC HOSE

B

C

NO METAL FRAMING AT REAR EDGE OF COCKPIT HOOD

BOUNDARY LAYER EXITS

RADAR COOLING CONNECTION

SLING & TRESTLE HERE

BRAKE CHARGING

WING PIN JOINT

SLING HERE

F

DATUM

RED

ENGINE MOUNTING

ELECTRICAL CONNECTIONS

VIEW OF TAIL FAIRING RUDDER REMOVED

BLACK

TAIL LIGHT

▲ **Wing cross-section, F Mk 5**

F

COLOUR LINES

◄ **Plan view, F Mk 5**
Port side

De Havilland Sea Venom F(AW) Mks 20 and 21

Country of origin: Great Britain.
Type: Two-seat, carrier-based, all-weather fighter and fighter-bomber.
Dimensions: Wing span 42ft 10in *13.06m*; length 36ft 8in *11.18m*; height 8ft 6¼in *2.60m*; wing area 279.8 sq ft *26.0m²*.
Weights: Loaded 15,800lb *7165kg*.

Powerplant: One De Havilland Ghost 105 turbojet of 5300lb *2403kg* static thrust.
Performance: Maximum speed 575mph *926kph* at sea level; initial climb rate 5900ft/min *1800m/min*; service ceiling 40,000ft *12,190m*; range 705 miles *1135km*.

Armament: Four fixed 20mm Hispano cannon, plus (optional) eight 60lb *27kg* rockets or up to 2000lb *907kg* of bombs.
Service: First flight 22 April 1954; service entry late 1954.

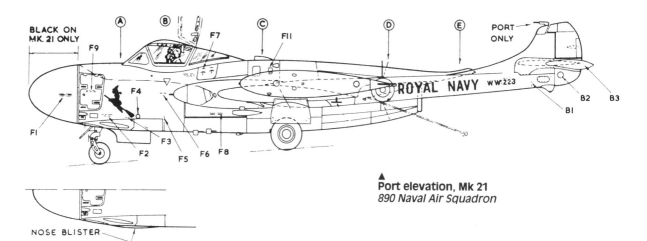

▲
Port elevation, Mk 21
890 Naval Air Squadron

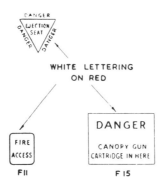

Stencilled instructions

B1 – Trestle. **B2** – Electrical connections. **B3** – NO PUSH. **F1** – Pull out radome before hingeing (Yellow). **F2** – Ground supply 28 volts (Yellow). **F3** – Plumb bob. **F4** – Pull step. **F5** – Trestle. **F6** – Keep off (Red). **F7** – First aid. Pull out and turn (Red). **F8** – Hydraulic pressure release valve inside. **F9** – Side door must be open before radome is closed. **F10** – Canopy hatch operation. (Detailed instructions stencilled here) (Red). **W1** – KEEP OFF (Red).

Sea Venom F(AW) Mk 21 of 890 NAS, the subject of our drawings. Note witch emblem on nose.
▼

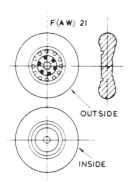

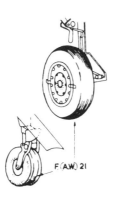

▲▶
Scrap views, Mk 21
Undercarriage details

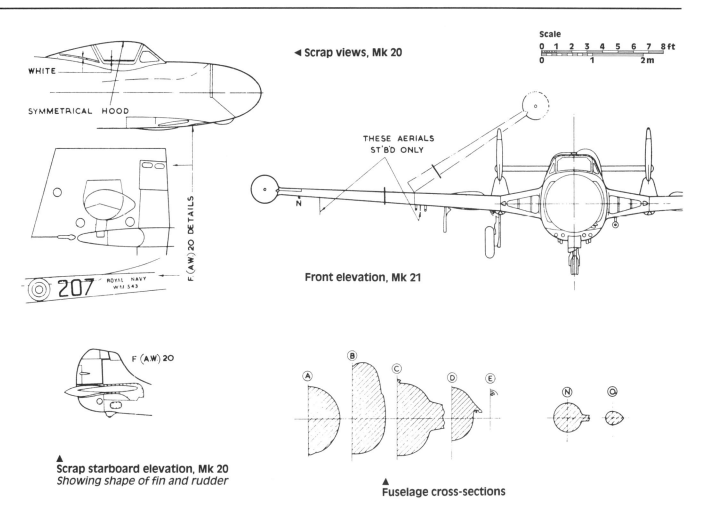

◄ Scrap views, Mk 20

WHITE

SYMMETRICAL HOOD

F (A.W.) 20 DETAILS

207   ROYAL NAVY
WM 543

Scale
0 1 2 3 4 5 6 7 8 ft
0   1   2 m

THESE AERIALS
ST'B'D ONLY

N

Front elevation, Mk 21

F (A.W.) 20

▲
Scrap starboard elevation, Mk 20
Showing shape of fin and rudder

A B C D E   N O

▲
Fuselage cross-sections

ROYAL NAVY   WW223

▲ Factory-fresh F(AW).21. Note arrangement of whip aerials and prominent tyre creep marks.

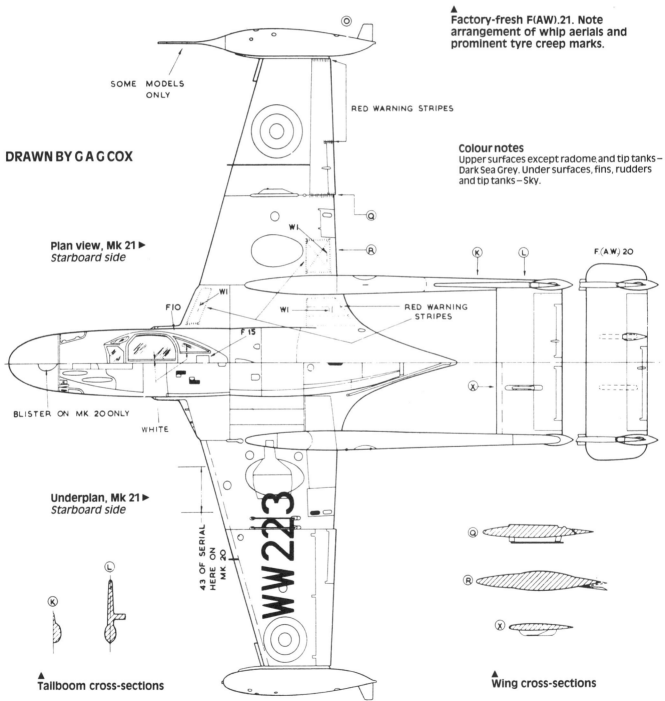

SOME MODELS ONLY

RED WARNING STRIPES

DRAWN BY G A G COX

Colour notes
Upper surfaces except radome and tip tanks – Dark Sea Grey. Under surfaces, fins, rudders and tip tanks – Sky.

Plan view, Mk 21 ▶
Starboard side

F(A.W.) 20

WI

Q

R

K   L

WI

WI

F 10

F 15

RED WARNING STRIPES

BLISTER ON MK 20 ONLY

X

WHITE

Underplan, Mk 21 ▶
Starboard side

43 OF SERIAL HERE ON MK 20

Q

R

WW223

X

L

K

▲ Tailboom cross-sections

▲ Wing cross-sections

Dassault Mystère IVA, B and N

Country of origin: France.
Type: Single-seat, land-based fighter and ground-attack aircraft.
Dimensions: Wing span 36ft 5¾in *11.12m*; length 42ft 2in *12.85m*, (IVB) 43ft 11½in *13.40m*, (IVN) 48ft 6in *14.80m*; height 14ft 5in *4.40m*; wing area 344.4 sq ft *32.0m²*.
Weights: Empty 12,524lb *5680kg*; loaded

16,317lb *7400kg*.
Powerplant: One Hispano-Suiza Verdon (Rolls-Royce Tay) turbojet of 7720lb *3500kg* thrust, (IVB, IVN) Rolls-Royce Avon RA7R afterburning turbojet of 9500lb *4308kg* static thrust.
Performance: Maximum speed (IVA) 695mph *1120kph* at sea level; service ceiling (IVA) 49,210ft *15,000m*; range (IVA,

clean) 570 miles *920km*.
Armament: Two fixed 30mm DEFA cannon and internal Matra pack with 55 rockets, plus (optional) up to 4000lb *1814kg* of external ordnance.
Service: First flight (IVA prototype) 28 September 1952, (IVB prototype) 16 December 1953, (IVN prototype) 19 July 1954; service entry (IVA) late 1954.

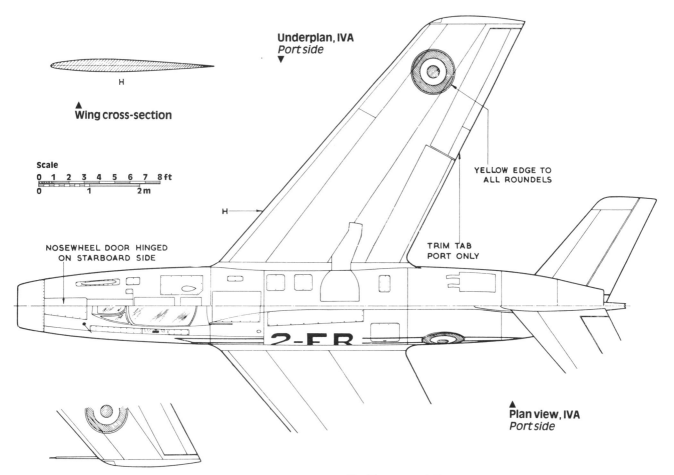

Wing cross-section

Scale

Underplan, IVA
Port side

YELLOW EDGE TO
ALL ROUNDELS

NOSEWHEEL DOOR HINGED
ON STARBOARD SIDE

TRIM TAB
PORT ONLY

Plan view, IVA
Port side

Mystère IVAs of the French Air Force with hastily applied yellow and black 'Suez stripes'.

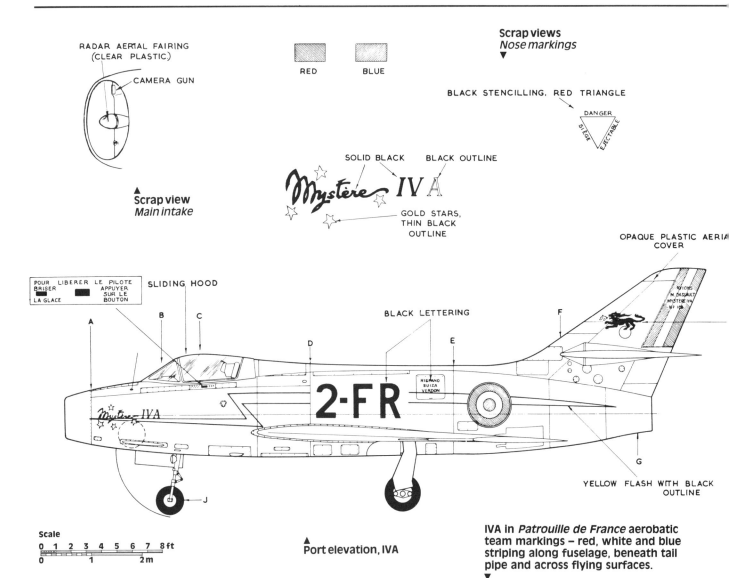

RADAR AERIAL FAIRING
(CLEAR PLASTIC)

CAMERA GUN

RED   BLUE

BLACK STENCILLING, RED TRIANGLE

DANGER
SIÈGE EJECTABLE

▲ Scrap view
Main intake

SOLID BLACK   BLACK OUTLINE

Mystère IVA

GOLD STARS,
THIN BLACK
OUTLINE

OPAQUE PLASTIC AERIAL
COVER

POUR LIBERER LE PILOTE
BRISER   APPUYER
LA GLACE   SUR LE
              BOUTON

SLIDING HOOD

BLACK LETTERING

AVIONS
M. DASSAULT
MYSTÈRE IVA
Nº 105

A   B   C   D   E   F

HISPANO
SUIZA
VERDON

2-FR

J

G

YELLOW FLASH WITH BLACK
OUTLINE

Scale
0 1 2 3 4 5 6 7 8 ft
0   1   2 m

▲ Port elevation, IVA

IVA in *Patrouille de France* aerobatic
team markings – red, white and blue
striping along fuselage, beneath tail
pipe and across flying surfaces.
▼

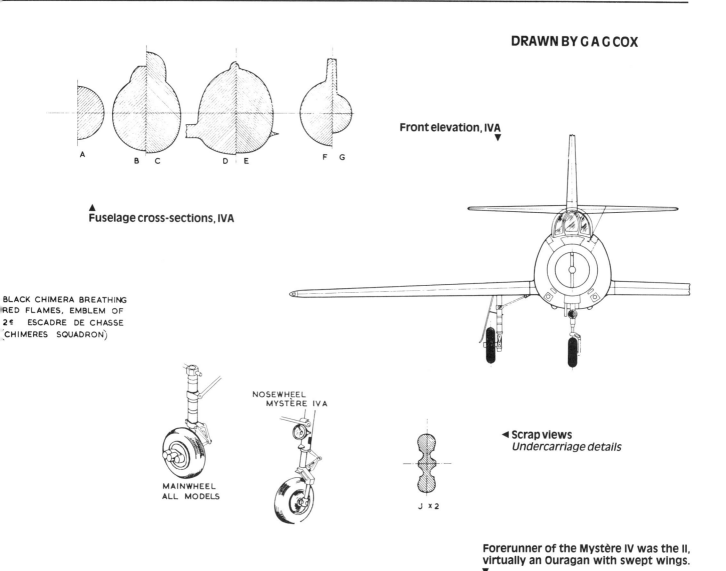

Fuselage cross-sections, IVA

Front elevation, IVA
▼

BLACK CHIMERA BREATHING
RED FLAMES, EMBLEM OF
2ᵉ ESCADRE DE CHASSE
(CHIMERES SQUADRON)

NOSEWHEEL
MYSTÈRE IVA

MAINWHEEL
ALL MODELS

J x 2

◄ Scrap views
Undercarriage details

**Forerunner of the Mystère IV was the II,
virtually an Ouragan with swept wings.**
▼

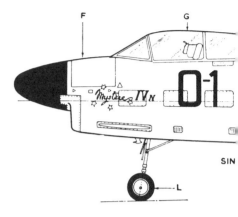

◄ 'Mystère de Nuit' (III), used for radar trials, with side-mounted main intakes, wing-tip pods and tandem seating.

SIN

▲
Mystère IVN, with nose radar, Sabre-like chin intake and extended, afterburning tail pipe.

NOSEWHEEL IVB
AND IVN

Scale
0 1 2 3 4 5 6 7 8 ft
0   1   2 m

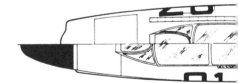

Fuselage cross-sections, IVB, IVN
▼

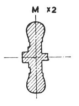

▲
Wheel cross-sections

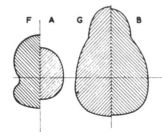

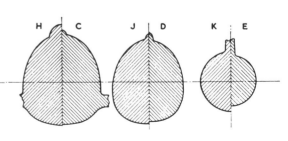

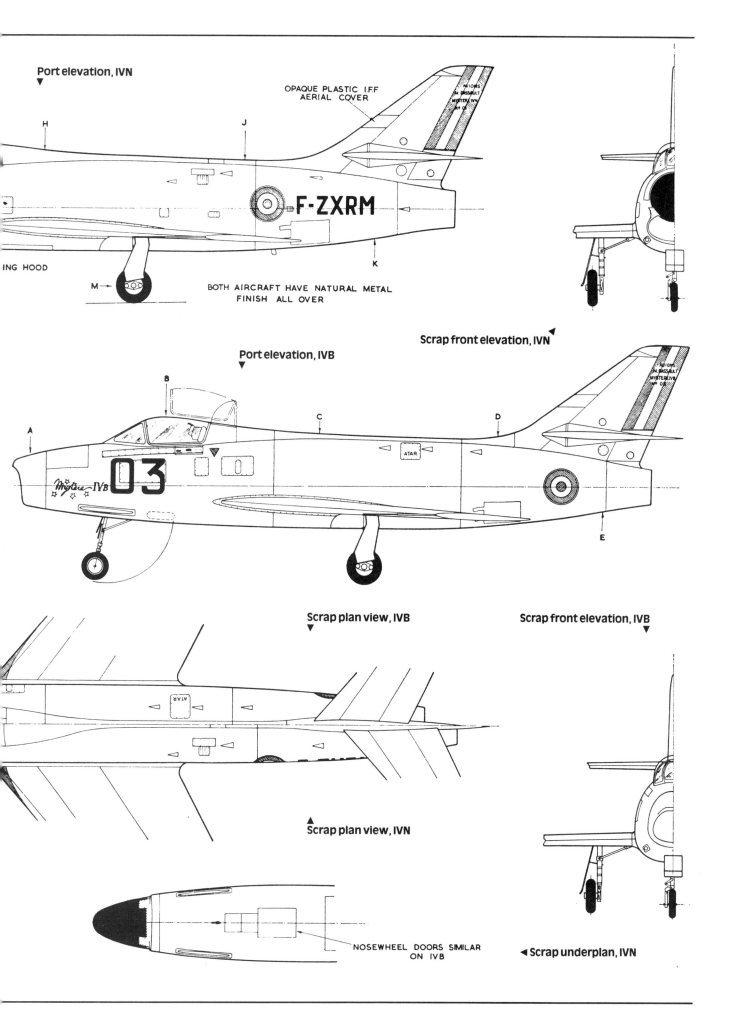

Port elevation, IVN
▼

OPAQUE PLASTIC I.F.F
AERIAL COVER

H

J

F-ZXRM

ING HOOD

M →

BOTH AIRCRAFT HAVE NATURAL METAL
FINISH ALL OVER

K

Scrap front elevation, IVN
◤

Port elevation, IVB
▼

B

C

D

A

03

Mystère-IVB

ATAR

E

Scrap plan view, IVB
▼

Scrap front elevation, IVB
▼

ATAR

Scrap plan view, IVN
▲

NOSEWHEEL DOORS SIMILAR
ON IVB

◄ **Scrap underplan, IVN**

Miles M77 Sparrowjet

Country of origin: Great Britain.
Type: Single-seat, land-based racing and research aircraft.
Dimensions: Wing span 28ft 8in *8.74m*; length 27ft 7in *8.42m*; height 5ft 6in

1.68m.
Weights: Empty 1450lb *658kg*; loaded 2400lb *1088kg*.
Powerplant: Two Turboméca Palas turbojets each rated at 331lb *150kg*

static thrust.
Performance: Maximum speed 230mph *370kph*.
Armament: None.
Service: First flight 14 December 1953.

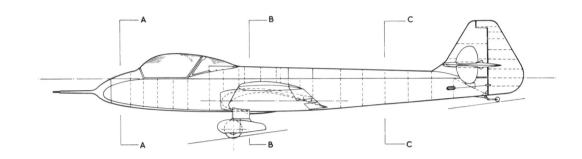

▲
Port elevation

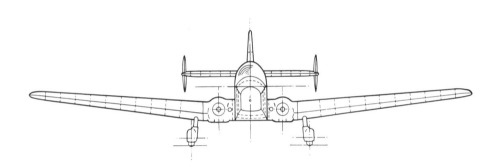

▲
Front elevation

Scale

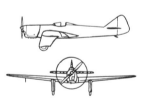

▲
Scrap views
Sparrowhawk for comparison

◄ Developed from the piston-engined Sparrowhawk, the M77 Sparrowjet was the first jet-powered racing aircraft to be produced in Britain.

Fuselage cross-sections
▼

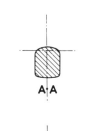

A·A

B·B

▲
The Sparrowjet prototype carried the same civil registration as the prototype Sparrowhawk, from which it was rebuilt.

C·C

◄ Plan view

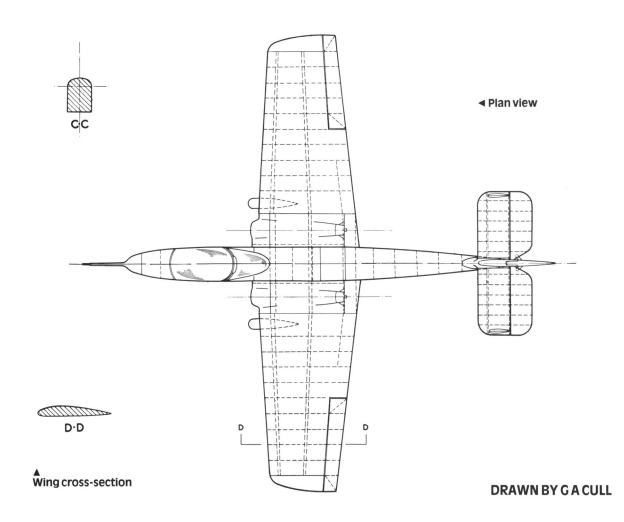

D·D

▲
Wing cross-section

DRAWN BY G A CULL

Leduc 021

Country of origin: France.
Type: Two-seat, air-launched, research aircraft.
Dimensions: Wing span 38ft 4½in *11.70m*; length 41ft 0in *12.50m*.

Weights: Loaded 11,470lb *5200kg*.
Powerplant: One Leduc ramjet of 16,535lb *7500kg* maximum thrust.
Performance: Maximum speed over 650mph *1050kph*; maximum climb rate

39,400ft/min *12,000m/min*; powered endurance 15min.
Armament: None.
Service: First flight 16 May 1953.

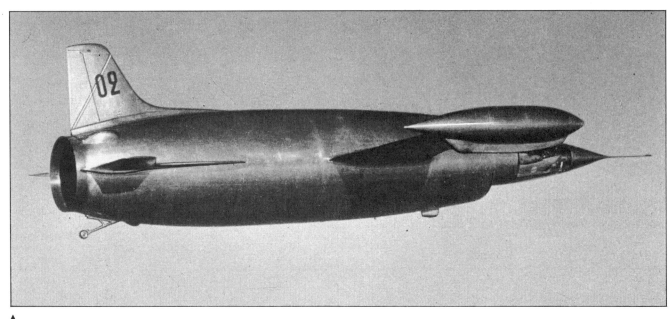

▲
The Leduc 021 was powered by a ramjet and had to be taken aloft 'pickaback' on a Languedoc 161 mother-ship.

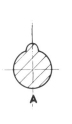
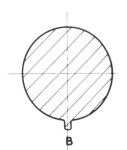
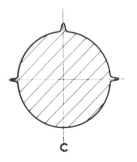
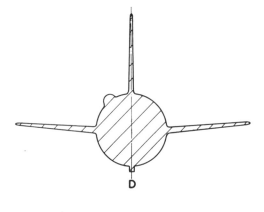

▲
Fuselage cross-sections

Wing and tailplane cross-sections
▼

◄ The transparent nose cone gave the pilot a remarkable view out of his pressurised cockpit, which projected from the centre of the annular main air intake.

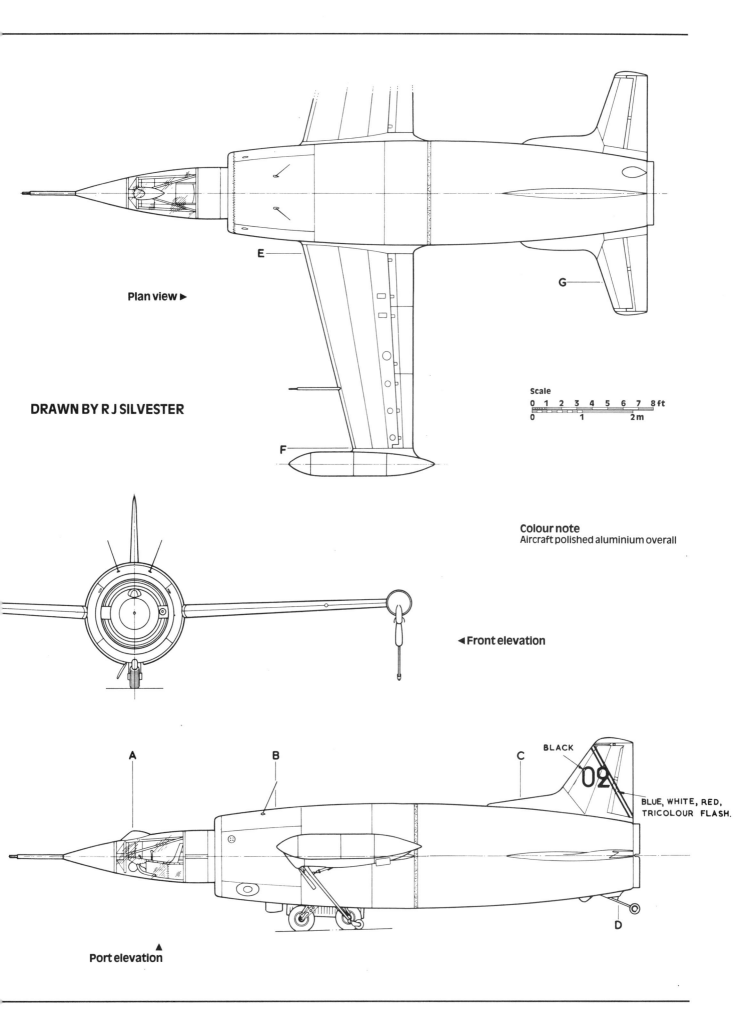

Plan view ►

DRAWN BY R J SILVESTER

E

G

F

Scale
0 1 2 3 4 5 6 7 8 ft
0 1 2 m

Colour note
Aircraft polished aluminium overall

◄Front elevation

A

B

C

BLACK

02

BLUE, WHITE, RED, TRICOLOUR FLASH.

D

▲
Port elevation

Hunting Percival Jet Provost T Mk 2

Country of origin: Great Britain.
Type: Two-seat, land-based trainer.
Dimensions: Wing span 35ft 2in *10.72m*; length 32ft 5in *9.88m*; height 10ft 2in *3.10m*; wing area 213.7 sq ft *19.85m²*.
Weights: Loaded about 6200lb *2810kg*.

Powerplant: One Armstrong Siddeley Viper Mk 9 axial-flow turbojet of 1750lb *794kg* static thrust.
Performance: Maximum speed 326mph *525kph* at 25,000ft *7620m*; initial climb rate 2400ft/min *730m/min*; service

ceiling over 40,000ft *12,190m*; range 565 miles *910km*.
Armament: None.
Service: First flight (Mk 1) 26 June 1954.

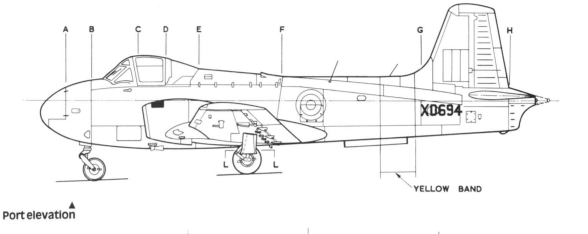

Port elevation ▲

YELLOW BAND

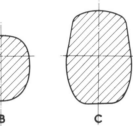 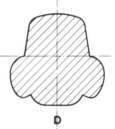 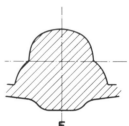 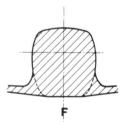

▲
Fuselage cross-sections

The last of ten Jet Provost Mk 1s, XD694, served as the prototype Mk 2. In its current, T Mk 5 guise the 'JP' is still fulfilling the role of *ab initio*/basic jet trainer for the RAF.
▼

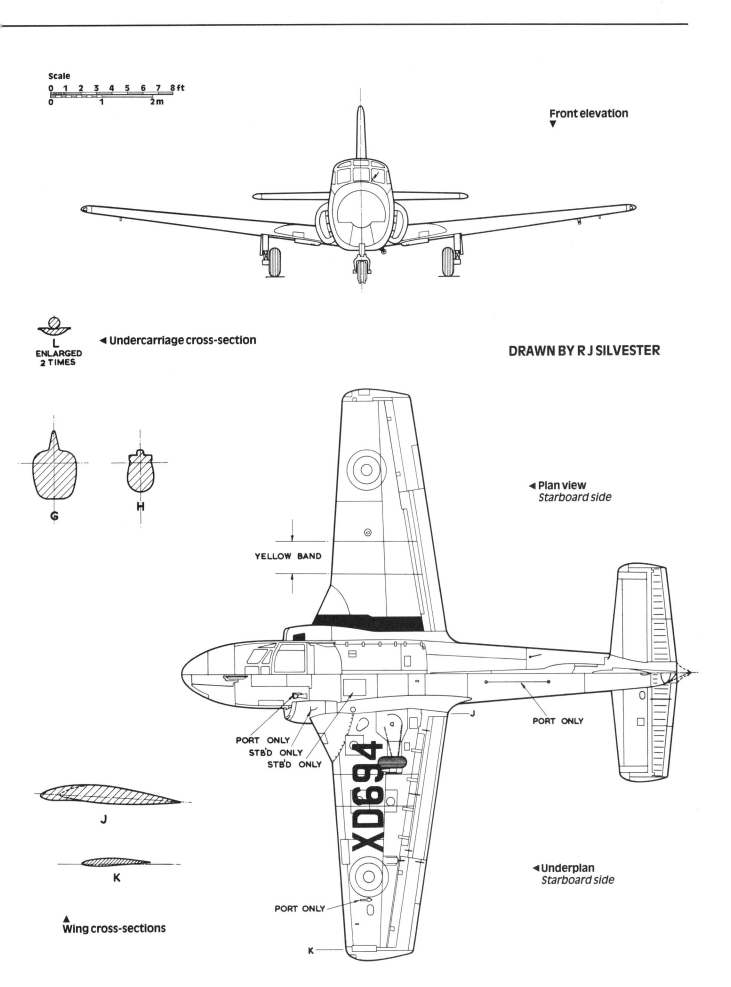

Scale
0 1 2 3 4 5 6 7 8 ft
0   1   2 m

Front elevation ▼

◄ Undercarriage cross-section

L
ENLARGED
2 TIMES

DRAWN BY R J SILVESTER

G   H

◄ **Plan view**
Starboard side

YELLOW BAND

J

PORT ONLY

PORT ONLY
STB'D ONLY
STB'D ONLY

J

PORT ONLY

XD694

K

PORT ONLY

◄ **Underplan**
Starboard side

K

▲
Wing cross-sections

Gloster Javelin F(AW) Mk 1

Country of origin: Great Britain.
Type: Two-seat, land-based, all-weather fighter.
Dimensions: Wing span 52ft 0in *15.85m*; length 56ft 9in *17.30m*; height 17ft 0in *5.18m*.
Powerplant: Two Armstrong Siddeley

Sapphire ASSa6 turbojets each of 8150lb *3696kg* thrust.
Performance: Maximum speed 530mph *853kph* at 35,000ft *10,670m*; initial climb rate 10,500ft/min *3200m/min*; service ceiling over 45,000ft *13,720m*; range (maximum external fuel) over 1000 miles

1600km.
Armament: Four fixed 30mm Aden cannon.
Service: First flight (prototype) 26 November 1951, (F(AW) Mk 1) 22 July 1954; service entry February 1956.

DRAWN BY G A G COX

Front elevation, Mk 1
▼

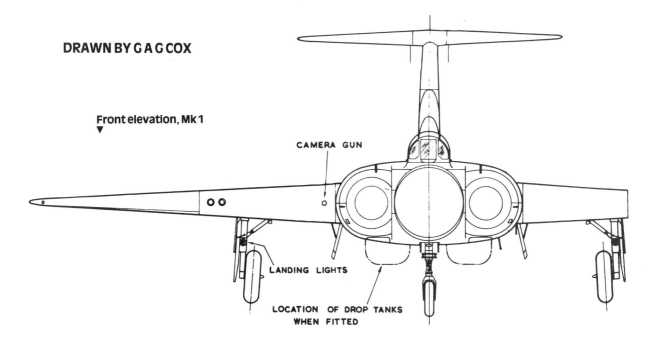

CAMERA GUN

LANDING LIGHTS

LOCATION OF DROP TANKS WHEN FITTED

XA620

WING SERIAL (X NEXT TO ROUNDEL)

Colour notes
Upper surfaces – Dark Green and Dark Sea Grey; under surfaces – silver. All lettering black unless otherwise stated.

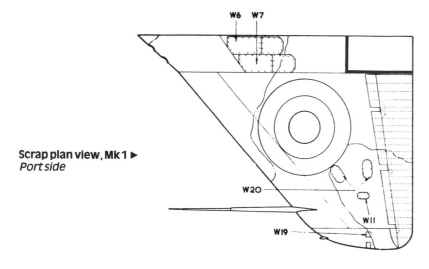

W6   W7

Scrap plan view, Mk 1 ▶
Port side

W20

W11

W19

FII FIO

Stencilled instructions (wing)
W1 – No 1 fuel tank. **W2** – No 2 fuel tank. **W3** – No 3 fuel tank. **W4** – No 4 fuel tank. **W5** – No 5 fuel tank. **W6** – Port inboard gun. **W7** – Port outboard gun. **W8** – Jacking point. **W9** – Outer wing attachment bolts. **W10** – Aileron controls. **W11** – Electrical. **W12** – Link collector box. **W13** – Aileron boost. **W14** – Trestle here. **W15** – Removal of U/C pivot pin. **W16** – Flap and airbrake jacks. **W17** – Airbrake jack. **W18** – Flap jack. **W19** – ILS aerial. **W20** – Aileron control inspection. **W21** – Fuel DRD 2482.

Scale

0 1 2 3 4 5 6 7 8 ft
0   1   2 m

▲ Gloster's big delta fighter saw widespread service in the RAF through the late 1950s and 1960s. This is an F(AW) Mk 2.

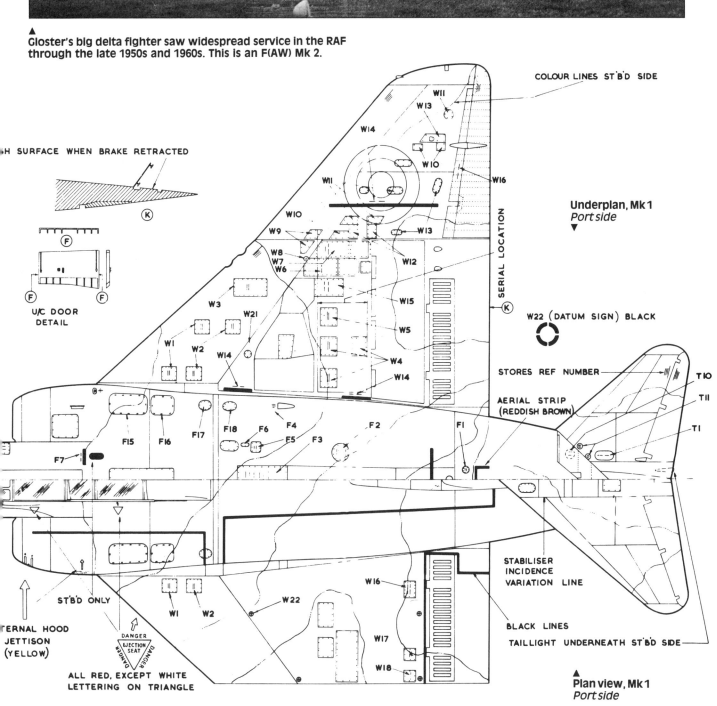

H SURFACE WHEN BRAKE RETRACTED

Ⓚ

Ⓕ

Ⓕ   Ⓕ

U/C DOOR
DETAIL

COLOUR LINES ST'B'D SIDE

WII
W13
W14
WIO
WII
WIO
W9
W8
W7
W6
W3
W21
W1   W2
W14
W13
W12
W15
W5
W4
W14
W16

SERIAL LOCATION

Ⓚ

Underplan, Mk 1
Port side
▼

W22 (DATUM SIGN) BLACK

STORES REF NUMBER   T10
AERIAL STRIP
(REDDISH BROWN)   T11
                                     T1

F15   F16   F17   F18   F6   F4   F2   F1
F7   F5   F3

STABILISER
INCIDENCE
VARIATION LINE

ST'B'D ONLY

ERNAL HOOD
JETTISON
(YELLOW)

DANGER
EJECTION
SEAT

ALL RED, EXCEPT WHITE
LETTERING ON TRIANGLE

W1   W2   W22

W16

W17

W18

BLACK LINES

TAILLIGHT UNDERNEATH ST'B'D SIDE

▲ **Plan view, Mk 1**
Port side

33

▲ Prototype Javelin T Mk 3, with lengthened fuselage, enlarged canopy and dual control (and, some would say, better looks!).

Scrap port elevation, T Mk 3
▼

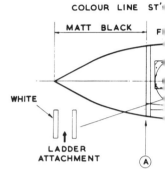

WHITE FRAMES ON IN
PERSPE

DA

ALL FRAMING

ALUMINIUM COLO

COLOUR LINE ST

MATT BLACK   F

WHITE

LADDER
ATTACHMENT

Ⓐ

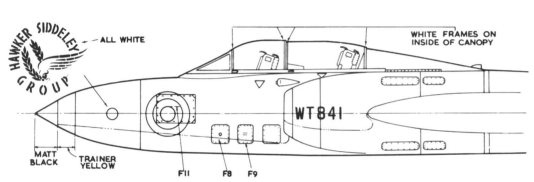

HAWKER SIDDELEY GROUP

— ALL WHITE

WHITE FRAMES ON
INSIDE OF CANOPY

WT841

MATT
BLACK

TRAINER
YELLOW

F11   F8   F9

Fuselage cross-sections, Mk 1 ▶

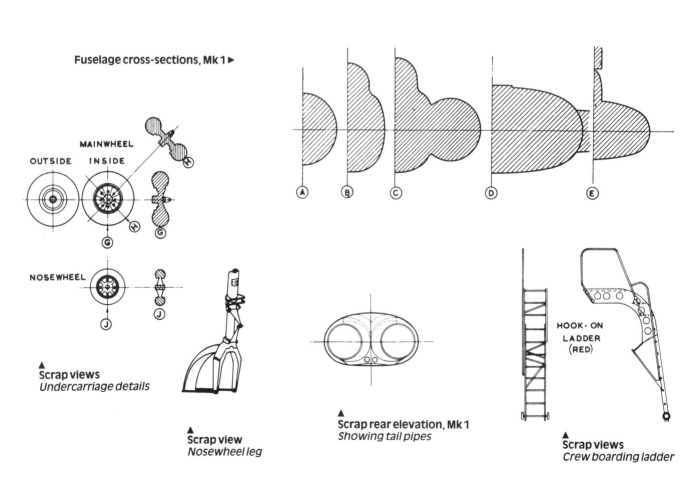

MAINWHEEL

OUTSIDE   INSIDE

H

G

G

H

NOSEWHEEL

J

J

Ⓐ   Ⓑ   Ⓒ   Ⓓ   Ⓔ

HOOK-ON
LADDER
(RED)

▲
Scrap views
Undercarriage details

▲
Scrap view
Nosewheel leg

▲
Scrap rear elevation, Mk 1
Showing tail pipes

▲
Scrap views
Crew boarding ladder

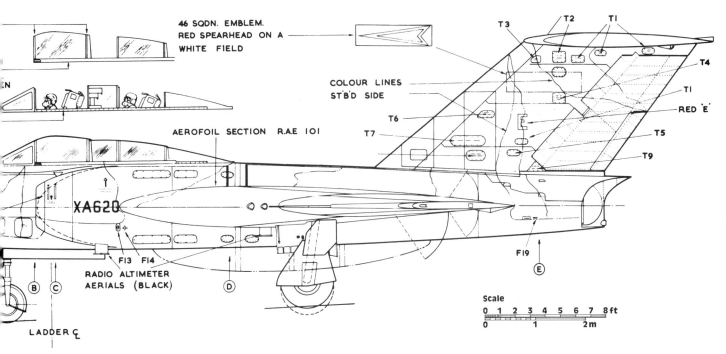

46 SQDN. EMBLEM.
RED SPEARHEAD ON A
WHITE FIELD

T3 T2 T1
T4
TI
RED 'E'
T5
T9

COLOUR LINES
ST'B'D SIDE

T6
T7

AEROFOIL SECTION R.A.E 101

XA620

F19

E

F13 F14
RADIO ALTIMETER
AERIALS (BLACK)

B C

D

LADDER C̹

Scale

0 1 2 3 4 5 6 7 8 ft

0   1   2 m

▲
Port elevation, Mk 1

Line-up of No 46 Squadron F(AW).1s at a rain-soaked Odiham, 1956, with Beverley transport beyond.
▼

Stencilled instructions (fuselage)

F1 – IFF aerial. F2 – Jet pipe attachment. Hot air manifold. Fuel drain and thermo-couple. F3 – Engine trunnions. Flying controls. Fuel filter and oil pump connections to engine oil tanks. F4 – Air cooling inlet. F5 – Engine control. F6 – Drop tank fuel lines. F7 – Trestle here. F8 – Oxygen bottles and cock. F9 – Survivor equipment. F10 – Nosewheel strut. F11 – AI equipment. F12 – (Censored). F13 – 28 volt ground supply. F14 – Air cooler duct. F15 – General services accumulator. F16 – Pacitor power unit gee and IFF receivers. F17 – No 1 fuselage tank. F18 – Aileron controls. F19 – Pull for step.

Stencilled instructions (tail)

T1 – Elevator layshaft. T2 – Tailplane jack motor. T3 – Tailplane motor. T4 – Elevator layshaft rudder trimmer box. T5 – Rudder locking gear. T6 – Hydraulics. T7 – Rudder boost unit. T8 – Rudder push rods. T9 – Lower rudder hinge. T10 – Tailplane seam attachment. T11 – WBH aerial run.

Convair F-102A Delta Dagger

Country of origin: USA.
Type: Single-seat, land-based, all-weather interceptor fighter.
Dimensions: Wing span 38ft 1½in *11.62m*; length 68ft 5in *20.85m*; height 21ft 2½in *6.46m*; wing area 661.5 sq ft *61.45m²*.
Weights: Empty 19,050lb *8639kg*; loaded 27,750lb *12,585kg*; maximum 31,500lb *14,285kg*.
Powerplant: One Pratt & Whitney J57-23 afterburning turbojet of 17,200lb *7800kg* thrust.
Performance: Maximum speed 825mph *1328kph* (Mach 1.25); initial climb rate 13,000ft/min *3960m/min*; service ceiling 54,000ft *16,460m*; range 1350 miles *2175km*.
Armament: Six AIM-4 Falcon AAMs in fuselage bay.
Service: First flight (YF-102) 24 October 1953, (YF-102A) 20 December 1954; service entry summer 1956.

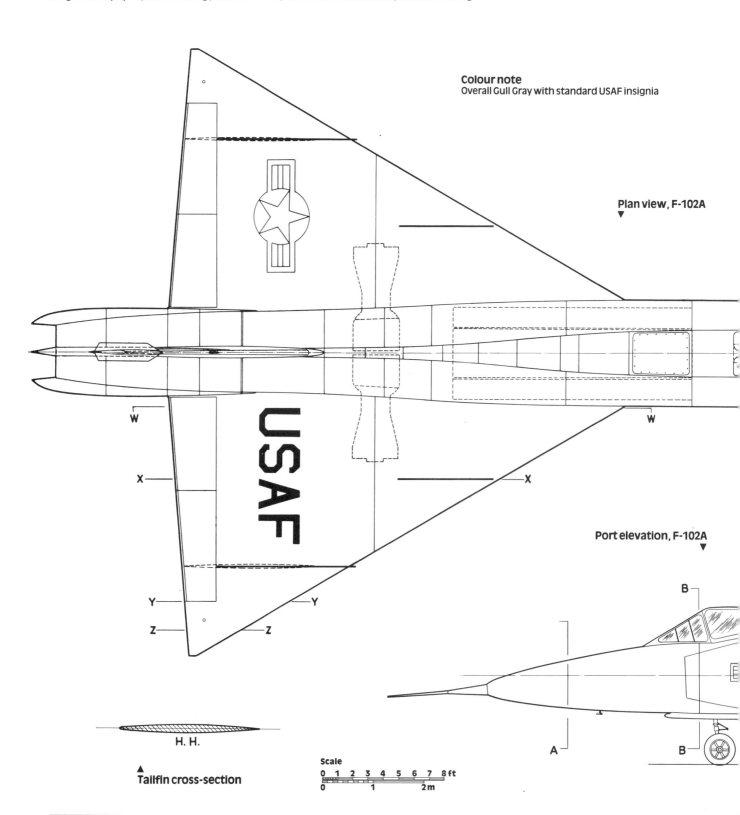

Colour note
Overall Gull Gray with standard USAF insignia

Plan view, F-102A
▼

Port elevation, F-102A
▼

H. H.

▲
Tailfin cross-section

Scale
0 1 2 3 4 5 6 7 8 ft
0   1   2 m

▲
Pre-production YF-102A, photographed in April 1955.
Production Delta Daggers showed new features, including
bigger air brakes aft of the tail fin.

Wing cross-sections
▼

W. W.

DRAWN BY J R ENOCH

X. X.

Y. Y.   Z. Z.

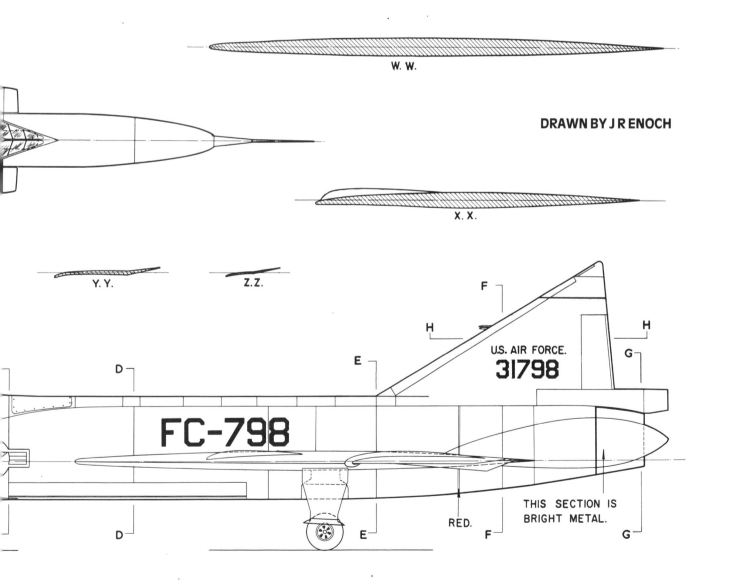

▲
**Landing gear almost retracted, 53-1787
is seen just after take-off.**

Fuselage cross-sections
▼►

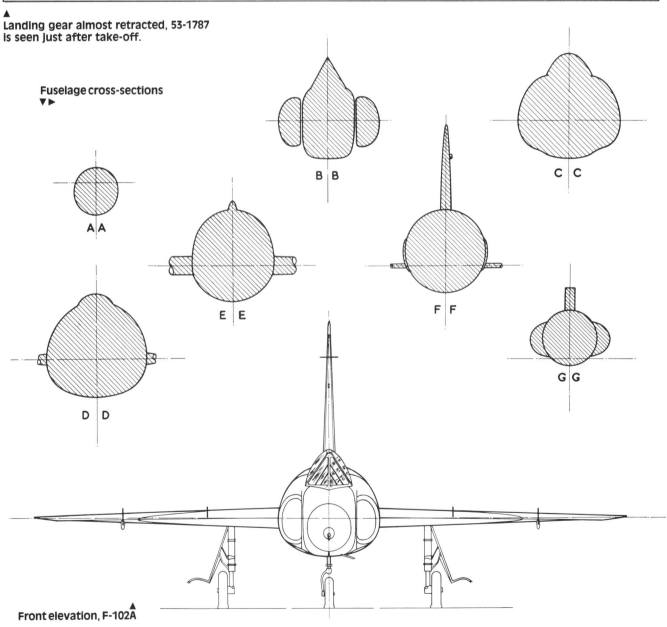

Front elevation, F-102A ▲

Grumman F9F-8 Cougar

Country of origin: USA.
Type: Single-seat, carrier-based fighter and fighter-bomber.
Dimensions: Wing span 34ft 6in *10.52m*; length 41ft 7in *12.68m*; height 12ft 3in *3.73m*; wing area 337 sq ft *31.31m²*.
Weights: Empty 13,000lb *5896kg*; normal loaded about 20,000lb *9070kg*.

Powerplant: One Pratt & Whitney J48-8 turbojet of 7000lb *3175kg* static thrust.
Performance: Maximum speed 712mph *1146kph*; initial climb rate 6100ft/min *1860m/min*; service ceiling 42,000ft *12,800m*; range (external fuel) 1100 miles *1770km*.
Armament: Four fixed 20mm M2 cannon,

plus (optional) six HVAR or four GAR-8 (Sidewinder) AAMs or four 1000lb *454kg* bombs.
Service: First flight (XF9F-6) 20 September 1951, (production -8) 18 January 1954; service entry 1955.

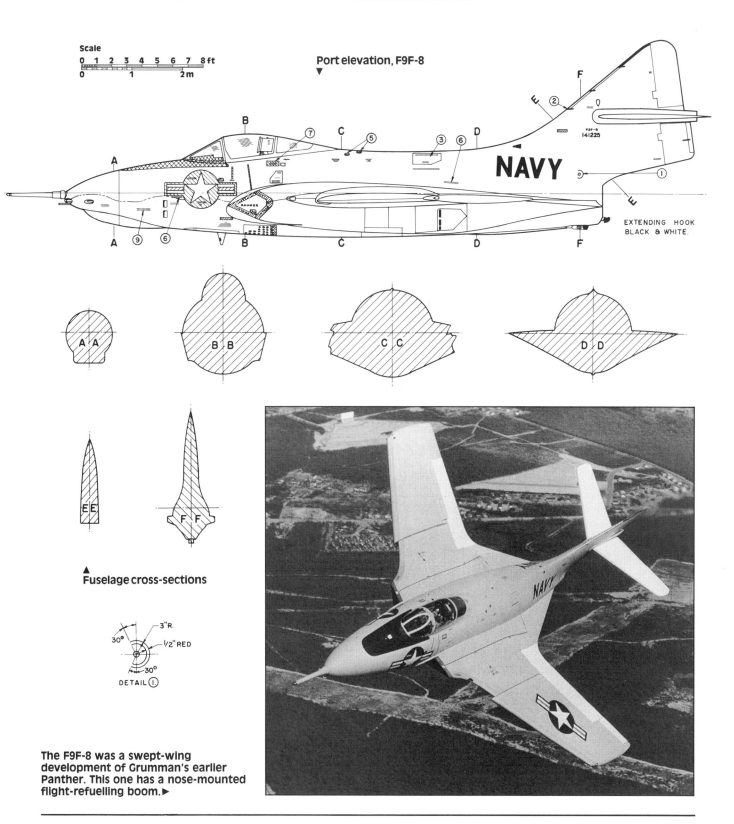

Scale
0 1 2 3 4 5 6 7 8ft
0 1 2m

Port elevation, F9F-8

NAVY

F9F-6
141225

EXTENDING HOOK
BLACK & WHITE.

A·A   B·B   C·C   D·D

E·E   F·F

▲
Fuselage cross-sections

3"R.
30°
½"RED
30°
DETAIL ①

The F9F-8 was a swept-wing development of Grumman's earlier Panther. This one has a nose-mounted flight-refuelling boom.▶

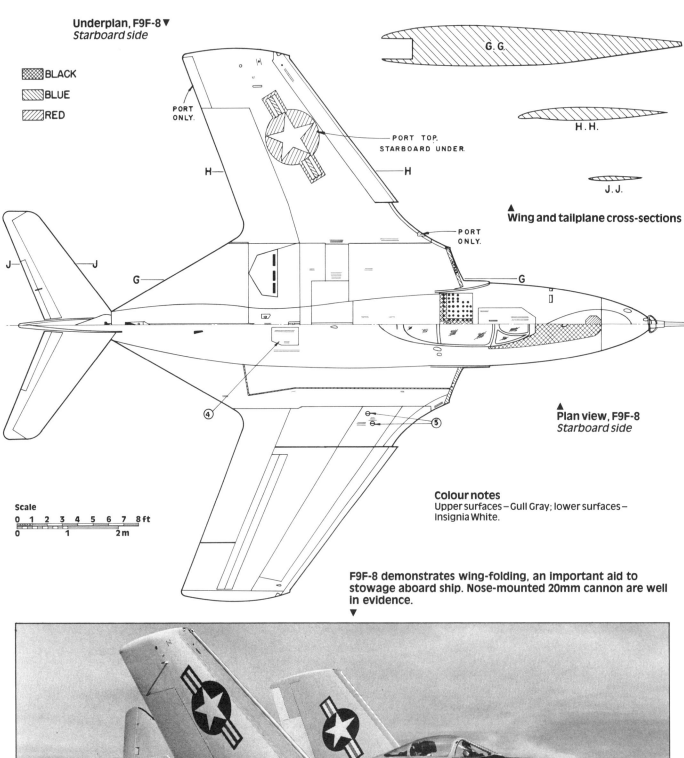

Underplan, F9F-8 ▼
Starboard side

⬛ BLACK
▨ BLUE
▨ RED

PORT ONLY.

PORT TOP. STARBOARD UNDER.

H

H

PORT ONLY.

J

J

G

G

④

⑤

G.G.

H.H.

J.J.

▲ Wing and tailplane cross-sections

▲ Plan view, F9F-8
Starboard side

Colour notes
Upper surfaces – Gull Gray; lower surfaces – Insignia White.

Scale

```
0  1  2  3  4  5  6  7  8 ft
0           1           2 m
```

F9F-8 demonstrates wing-folding, an important aid to stowage aboard ship. Nose-mounted 20mm cannon are well in evidence.
▼

▲
The F9F-8P was the photo-recce version of the Cougar and featured a lengthened front fuselage. It first flew in August 1955.

F9F-8P

▲
Scrap port elevation, F9F-8P

Scrap port elevation, F9F-8T
▼

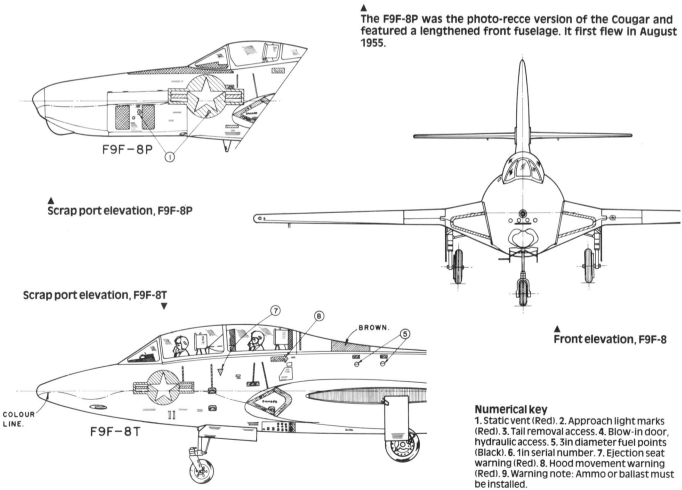

BROWN.

COLOUR LINE.

F9F-8T

▲
Front elevation, F9F-8

Numerical key
1. Static vent (Red). 2. Approach light marks (Red). 3. Tail removal access. 4. Blow-in door, hydraulic access. 5. 3in diameter fuel points (Black). 6. 1in serial number. 7. Ejection seat warning (Red). 8. Hood movement warning (Red). 9. Warning note: Ammo or ballast must be installed.

Fairey FD2

Country of origin: Great Britain.
Type: Single-seat, land-based research aircraft.
Dimensions: Wing span 26ft 10in *8.18m*; length overall 51ft 7½in *15.74m*; height 11ft 0in *3.35m*; wing area 360 sq ft *33.44m²*.

Weights: Empty equipped about 11,000lb *4990kg*; maximum about 13,500lb *6122kg*.
Powerplant: One Rolls-Royce Avon RA5 afterburning turbojet of about 12,000lb *5442kg* static thrust.
Performance: Maximum speed 1130mph

1820kph (Mach 1.7) at altitude; initial climb rate 15,000ft/min *4570m/min*; service ceiling over 40,000ft *12,190m*; range 830 miles *1335km*.
Armament: None.
Service: First flight 6 October 1954.

Colour notes
Polished metal on all surfaces; standard RAF Type 'D' roundels and fin flashes; black anti-dazzle on nose.

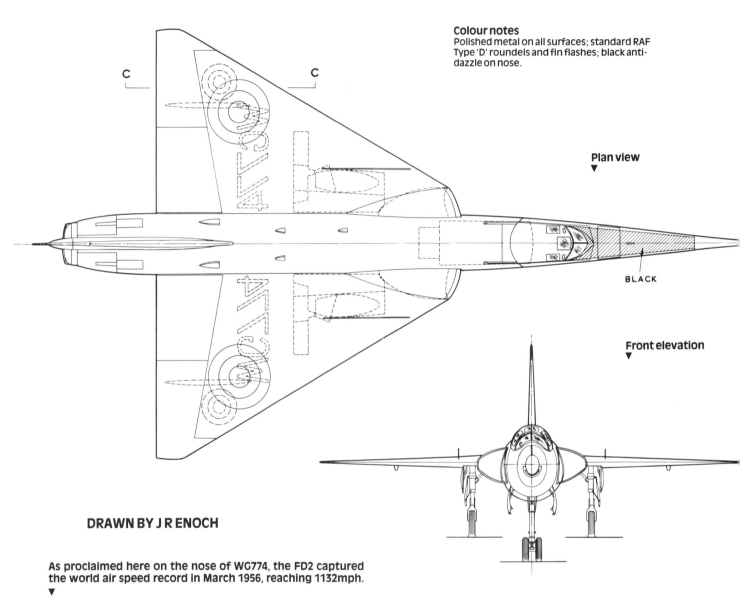

Plan view ▼

BLACK

Front elevation ▼

DRAWN BY J R ENOCH

As proclaimed here on the nose of WG774, the FD2 captured the world air speed record in March 1956, reaching 1132mph.
▼

Scale
0 1 2 3 4 5 6 7 8 ft
0   1   2 m

▲
WG777 was the second and last FD2. The design 'borrowed' P.1 (Lightning) main wheels and Gannet nose gear. Note roundel on top of fuselage.

Fuselage cross-sections
▼

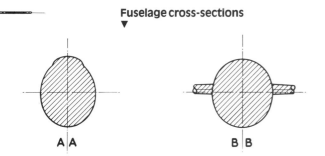

A|A   B|B

C C

▲
Wing cross-section

▲
Head-on view of WG777. This FD2 carried a mauve paint finish.

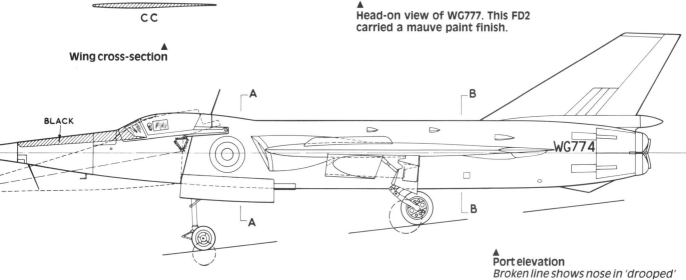

▲
Port elevation
Broken line shows nose in 'drooped' position

Sud-Est SE5003 Baroudeur

Country of origin: France.
Type: Prototype single-seat, land-based fighter.
Dimensions: Wing span 32ft 9½in *10.00m*; length 44ft 3in *13.49m*; height (including trolley) 11ft 9½in *3.60m*.

Powerplant: One SNECMA Atar 101E-3 axial-flow turbojet of 7717lb *3500kg* static thrust.
Performance: Maximum speed 683mph *1100kph* at sea level; time to 40,000ft *12,190m*, 6.8min.

Armament: Two fixed 30mm cannon, plus up to 2200lb *1000kg* of external ordnance.
Service: First flight (SE.5000/01) 1 August 1953, (SE.5003/01) May 1956.

Port elevation, 3rd pre-production aircraft
Dotted circles indicate position of trolley wheels
▼

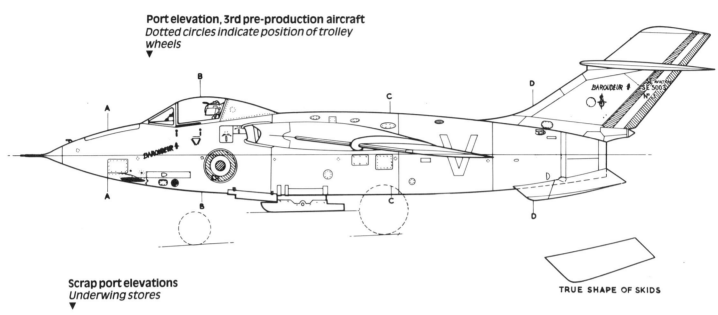

Scrap port elevations
Underwing stores
▼

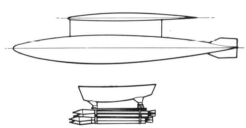

TRUE SHAPE OF SKIDS

Fuselage cross-sections ▼

A A

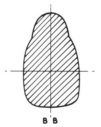

B B

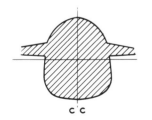

C C

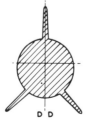

D D

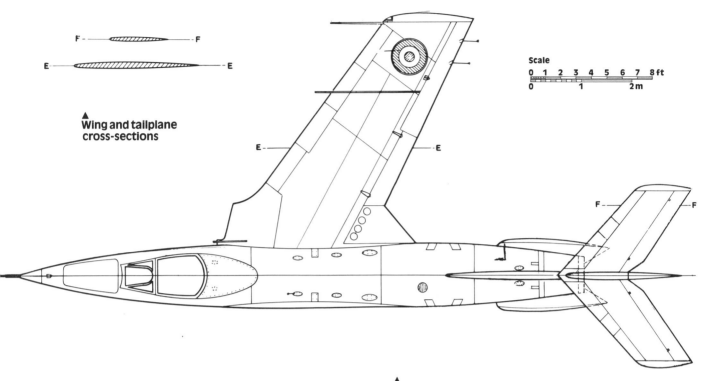

F — F

E — E

▲ Wing and tailplane
cross-sections

E — E

F — F

Scale

0 1 2 3 4 5 6 7 8 ft

0 1 2 m

▲
Plan view, 3rd pre-production aircraft

Second pre-production Baroudeur in wintry surroundings,
offering a good view of the landing skid arrangement. The
designer of this unique aircraft was W J Jakimiuk, formerly
chief designer at PZL in Poland and subsequently
responsible for the Chipmunk trainer.
▼

DRAWN BY M A BADROCKE

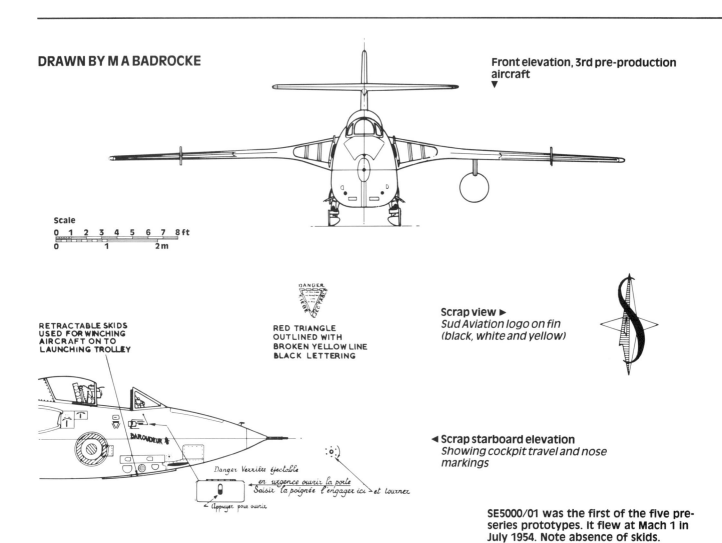

Front elevation, 3rd pre-production aircraft
▼

Scale
0 1 2 3 4 5 6 7 8 ft
0   1   2 m

DANGER

RETRACTABLE SKIDS
USED FOR WINCHING
AIRCRAFT ON TO
LAUNCHING TROLLEY

RED TRIANGLE
OUTLINED WITH
BROKEN YELLOW LINE
BLACK LETTERING

BAROUDEUR

Danger Verrière éjectable
en urgence ouvrir la porte
Saisir la poignée l'engager ici et tourner
Appuyer pour ouvrir

Scrap view ►
*Sud Aviation logo on fin
(black, white and yellow)*

◄ Scrap starboard elevation
*Showing cockpit travel and nose
markings*

SE5000/01 was the first of the five pre-series prototypes. It flew at Mach 1 in July 1954. Note absence of skids.
▼

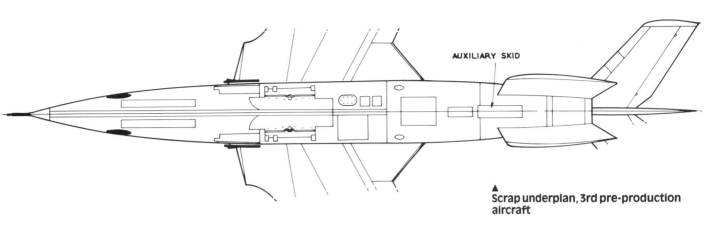

▲
Scrap underplan, 3rd pre-production aircraft

AUXILIARY SKID

▲
Third pre-production aircraft, subject of the plans, with retractable rear skid deployed.

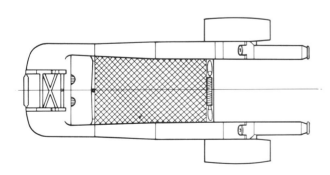

Rocket propelled take-off trolley ▲
Plan view, front elevation and port elevation

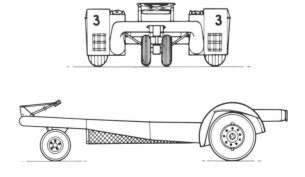

Chance Vought F8U-1 and -3 Crusader

Country of origin: USA.
Type: Single-seat, carrier-based fighter.
Dimensions: (F8U-1) Wing span 35ft 8in *10.87m*; length 54ft 3in *16.54m*; height 15ft 9in *4.80m*; wing area 375 sq ft *34.84m²*.
Weights: (-1) Normal take-off 27,000lb *12,245kg*; maximum 34,000lb *15,420kg*.

Powerplant: (-1) One Pratt & Whitney J57-12 afterburning turbojet of 11,200lb *5080kg* thrust.
Performance: (-1) Maximum speed 1013mph *1631kph* (Mach 1.54) at altitude; initial climb rate 20,000ft/min *6100m/ min*; service ceiling 50,000ft *15,240m*; range 1200 miles *1930km*.

Armament: Four fixed 20mm Colt cannon, plus two AAM-N-7 (Sidewinder) AAMs and 32 FFAR in belly pack.
Service: First flight (XF8U-1) 25 March 1955, (F8U-1) November 1956; service entry (-1) 25 March 1957.

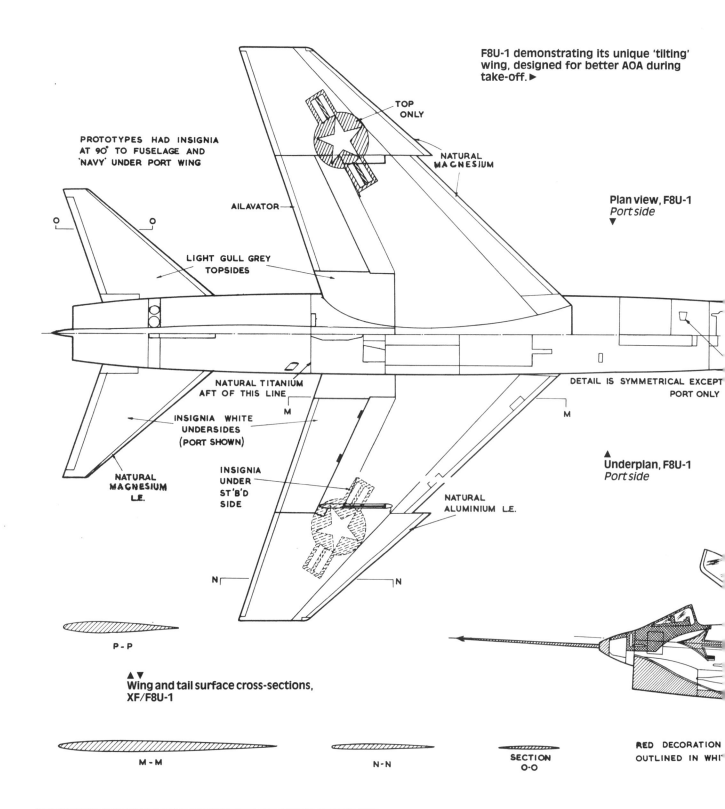

F8U-1 demonstrating its unique 'tilting' wing, designed for better AOA during take-off. ▶

TOP ONLY

PROTOTYPES HAD INSIGNIA AT 90° TO FUSELAGE AND 'NAVY' UNDER PORT WING

NATURAL MAGNESIUM

AILAVATOR

LIGHT GULL GREY TOPSIDES

Plan view, F8U-1
Port side ▼

NATURAL TITANIUM AFT OF THIS LINE

M

DETAIL IS SYMMETRICAL EXCEPT PORT ONLY

M

INSIGNIA WHITE UNDERSIDES (PORT SHOWN)

NATURAL MAGNESIUM L.E.

INSIGNIA UNDER ST'B'D SIDE

NATURAL ALUMINIUM L.E.

▲ Underplan, F8U-1
Port side

N   N

P - P

▲▼
Wing and tail surface cross-sections, XF/F8U-1

M - M   N-N   SECTION O-O

RED DECORATION OUTLINED IN WHI'

Scale
0 1 2 3 4 5 6 7 8 ft
0   1   2 m

▲
Scrap view
Wing-fold detail

◫ RED ◩ BLUE ▨ DARK GREEN ■ BLACK ☐ WHITE STAR & RECTANGLES IN INSIGNIA

Port elevation, XF8U-1
▼

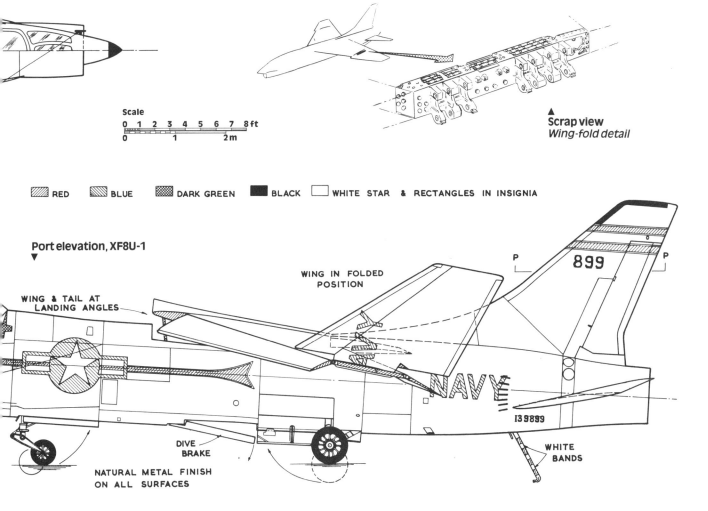

WING & TAIL AT
LANDING ANGLES

WING IN FOLDED
POSITION

P   899   P

NAVY

139899

WHITE
BANDS

DIVE
BRAKE

NATURAL METAL FINISH
ON ALL SURFACES

▲ Prototype XF8U-1, as drawn on previous spread, showing the widely varying tones of its natural metal finish.

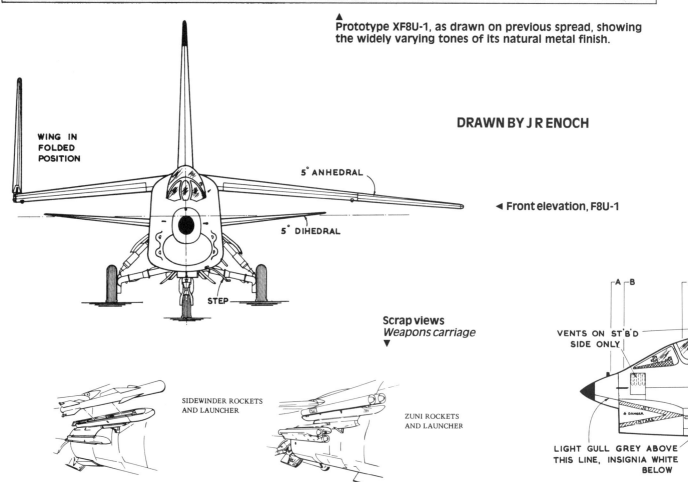

WING IN
FOLDED
POSITION

5° ANHEDRAL

5° DIHEDRAL

STEP

DRAWN BY J R ENOCH

◄ Front elevation, F8U-1

Scrap views
Weapons carriage
▼

SIDEWINDER ROCKETS
AND LAUNCHER

ZUNI ROCKETS
AND LAUNCHER

A ┌ B

VENTS ON ST'B'D
SIDE ONLY

LIGHT GULL GREY ABOVE
THIS LINE, INSIGNIA WHITE
BELOW

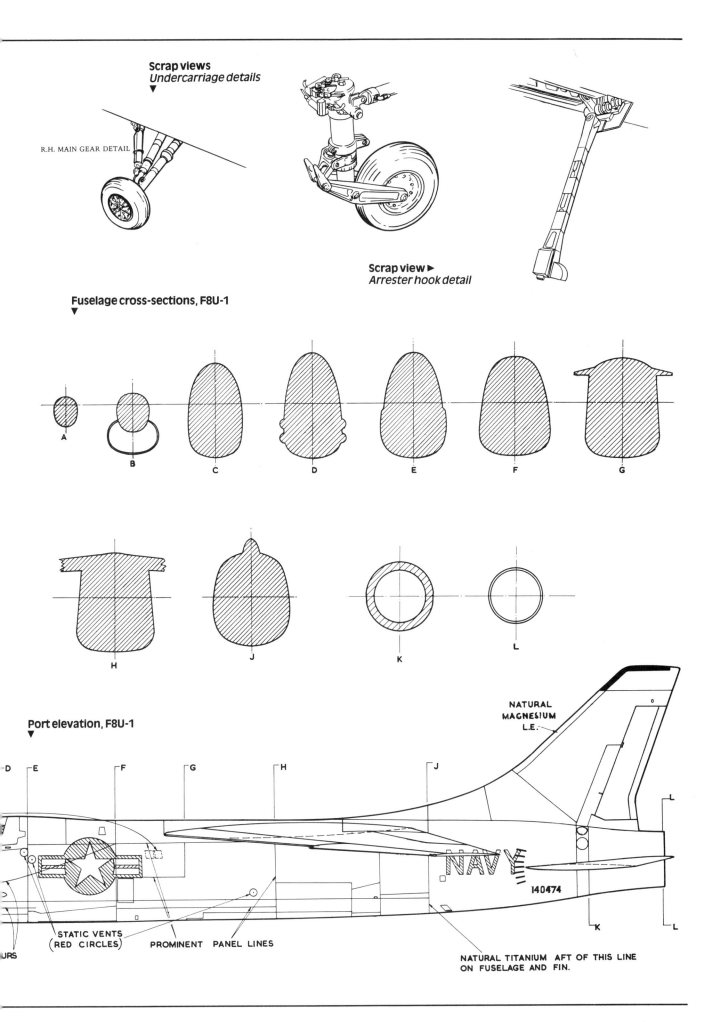

Scrap views
Undercarriage details
▼

R.H. MAIN GEAR DETAIL

Scrap view ▶
Arrester hook detail

Fuselage cross-sections, F8U-1
▼

A
B
C
D
E
F
G

H
J
K
L

Port elevation, F8U-1
▼

D E F G H J L

NATURAL
MAGNESIUM
L.E.

NAVY
140474

STATIC VENTS
(RED CIRCLES)

PROMINENT PANEL LINES

NATURAL TITANIUM AFT OF THIS LINE
ON FUSELAGE AND FIN.

URS

K L

Sidewinder-armed F8U-2N aboard *Forrestal*. In the 1962 USN reorganisation, Crusaders were redesignated F-8, this particular version becoming the F-8D.

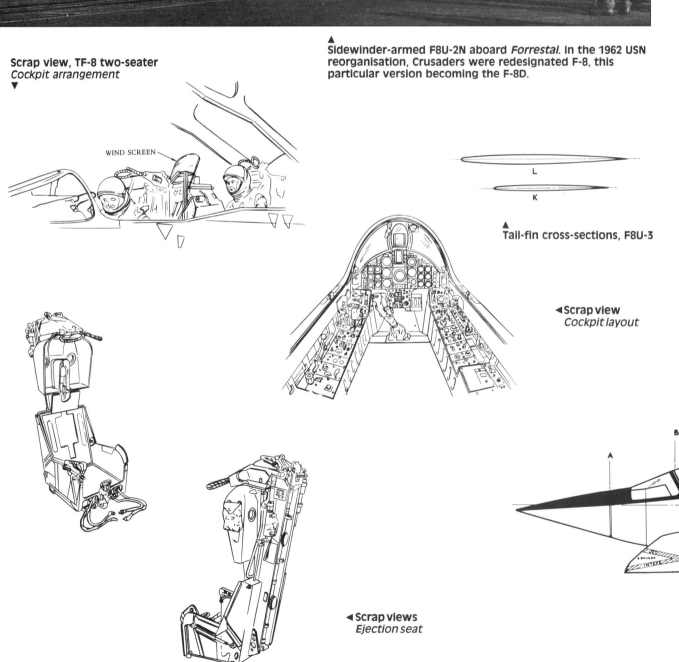

Scrap view, TF-8 two-seater
Cockpit arrangement
▼

WIND SCREEN

▲
Tail-fin cross-sections, F8U-3

L

K

◄ **Scrap view**
Cockpit layout

◄ **Scrap views**
Ejection seat

▲
F8U-1P photo-reconnaissance variant, first flight of which took place in late 1956, showing squared-off forward fuselage.

Fuselage cross-sections, F8U-3
▼

A   B   C   D   E   F   G   H   J

Port elevation, F8U-3
▼

6340

NAVY

F8U-3
146340

Scale

0 1 2 3 4 5 6 7 8 ft

0   1   2 m

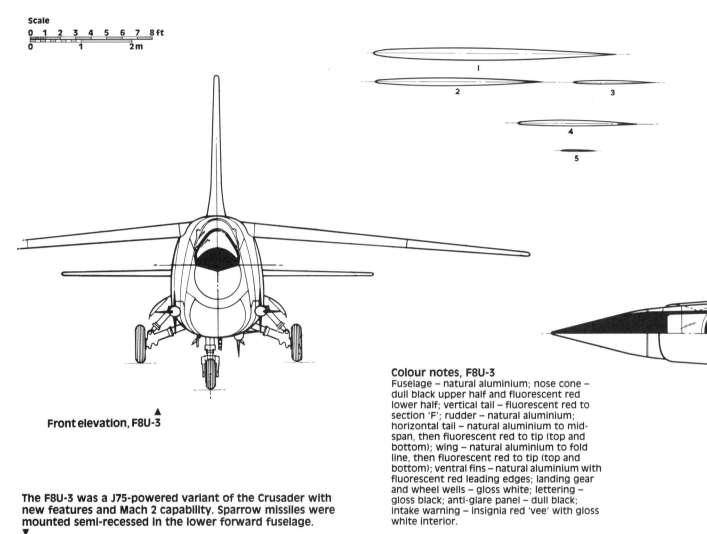

▲
Front elevation, F8U-3

Colour notes, F8U-3
Fuselage – natural aluminium; nose cone –
dull black upper half and fluorescent red
lower half; vertical tail – fluorescent red to
section 'F'; rudder – natural aluminium;
horizontal tail – natural aluminium to mid-
span, then fluorescent red to tip (top and
bottom); wing – natural aluminium to fold
line, then fluorescent red to tip (top and
bottom); ventral fins – natural aluminium with
fluorescent red leading edges; landing gear
and wheel wells – gloss white; lettering –
gloss black; anti-glare panel – dull black;
intake warning – insignia red 'vee' with gloss
white interior.

**The F8U-3 was a J75-powered variant of the Crusader with
new features and Mach 2 capability. Sparrow missiles were
mounted semi-recessed in the lower forward fuselage.**
▼

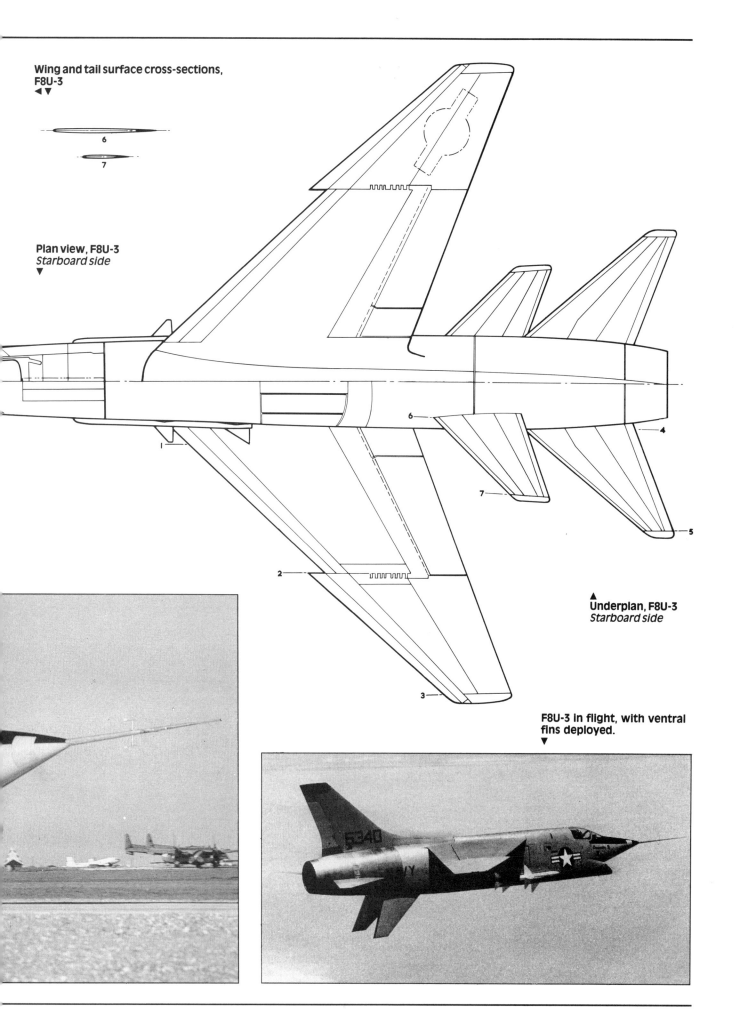

Wing and tail surface cross-sections, F8U-3
◀▼

6

7

Plan view, F8U-3
Starboard side
▼

▲
Underplan, F8U-3
Starboard side

F8U-3 in flight, with ventral fins deployed.
▼

Republic F-105B Thunderchief

Country of origin: USA.
Type: Single-seat, land-based fighter-bomber.
Dimensions: Wing span 34ft 11¼in *10.65m*; length 64ft 3in *19.58m*; height 19ft 8in *6.00m*; wing area 385 sq ft *35.77m²*.
Weights: Empty 23,900lb *10,840kg*; maximum 44,600lb *20,225kg*.

Powerplant: One Pratt & Whitney J75-5 afterburning turbojet of 23,500lb *10,660kg* thrust.
Performance: Maximum speed 1250mph *2010kph*; initial climb rate 34,000ft/min *10,365m/min*; service ceiling 52,000ft *15,850m*; range (maximum external fuel) 2400 miles *3860km*.

Armament: One fixed 20mm M61 cannon, plus up to 8000lb *3628kg* of bombs in fuselage bay and up to 6000lb *2720kg* of external ordnance.
Service: First flight (YF-105A) 22 October 1955, (F-105B) 26 May 1956; service entry (B) 27 May 1958.

DRAWN BY G A G COX

Scale

Front elevation ▼

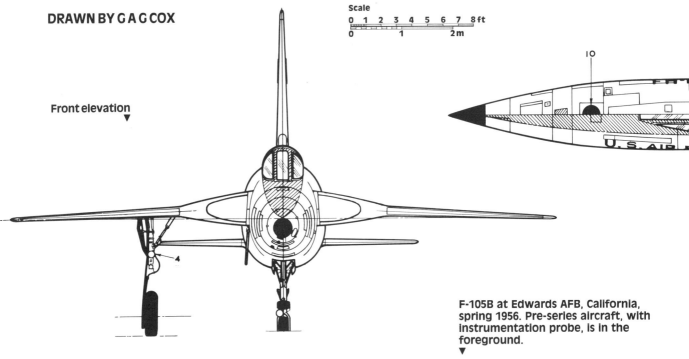

F-105B at Edwards AFB, California, spring 1956. Pre-series aircraft, with instrumentation probe, is in the foreground. ▼

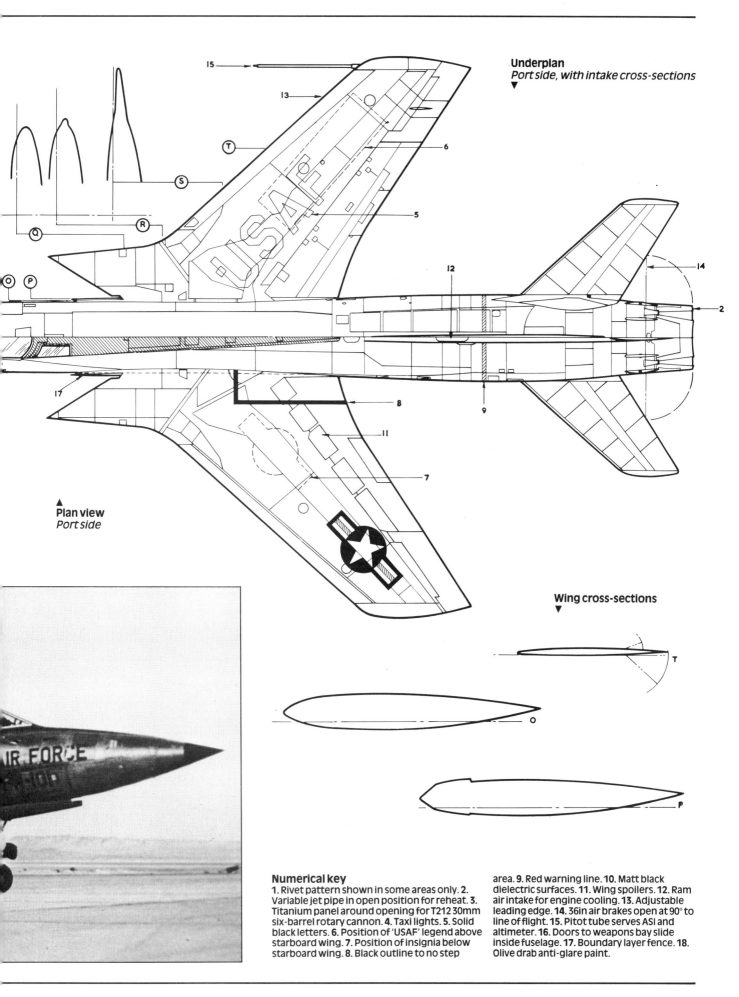

15

13

T

S

Q

R

6

O   P

5

12

14

2

17

8

9

11

7

▲
Plan view
Port side

Wing cross-sections
▼

T

O

P

Numerical key
1. Rivet pattern shown in some areas only. 2. Variable jet pipe in open position for reheat. 3. Titanium panel around opening for T212 30mm six-barrel rotary cannon. 4. Taxi lights. 5. Solid black letters. 6. Position of 'USAF' legend above starboard wing. 7. Position of insignia below starboard wing. 8. Black outline to no step area. 9. Red warning line. 10. Matt black dielectric surfaces. 11. Wing spoilers. 12. Ram air intake for engine cooling. 13. Adjustable leading edge. 14. 36in air brakes open at 90° to line of flight. 15. Pitot tube serves ASI and altimeter. 16. Doors to weapons bay slide inside fuselage. 17. Boundary layer fence. 18. Olive drab anti-glare paint.

▲
First-flight photo of the F-105B. The 'Thud' served with great distrinction during the Vietnam War, proving capable of absorbing tremendous punishment.

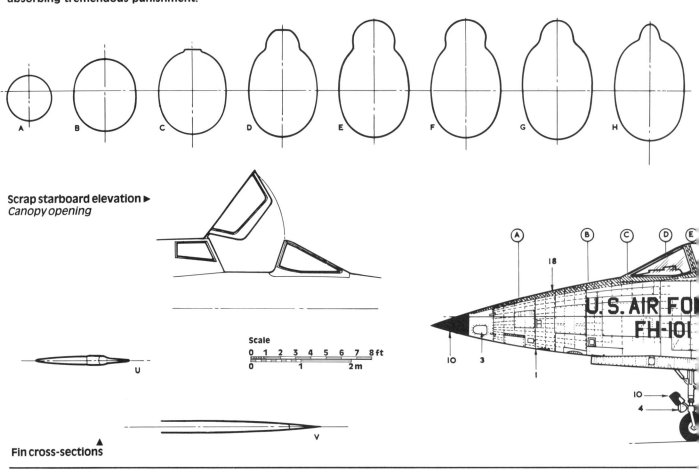

A B C D E F G H

Scrap starboard elevation ▶
Canopy opening

U

Scale
0 1 2 3 4 5 6 7 8 ft
0   1   2 m

V

▲
Fin cross-sections

A B C D E

18

U.S. AIR FO
FH-101

10
3
1

10
4

▲
**Thunderchief plus weapons options –
plus pilot!**

◄ **Fuselage cross-sections**

J   K   L   M   N

40101

F   G   H   J   K   U   V   M   N

16

L

▲ **Port elevation**

Hawker Siddeley Buccaneer S Mk 2

Country of origin: Great Britain.
Type: Two-seat, carrier-based (later land-based) strike aircraft.
Dimensions: Wing span 44ft 0in *13.41m*; length 63ft 5in *19.33m*; height 16ft 3in *4.95m*; wing area 515 sq ft *47.84m²*.
Weights: Empty about 30,000lb

13,600kg; maximum about 62,000lb *28,100kg*.
Powerplant: Two Rolls-Royce Spey Mk 101 turbofans each of 11,030lb *5000kg* thrust.
Performance: Maximum speed over 700mph *1125kph* at sea level; range

(typical) 2300 miles *1700km*.
Armament: Up to 4000lb *1814kg* of bombs in fuselage bay, plus up to 12,000lb *5440kg* of external ordnance.
Service: First flight (NA39) 30 April 1958, (prototype S Mk 2) 17 May 1963; service entry March 1965.

▲
XN974, the first Buccaneer S.2. Dramatic improvements in performance over the Gyron Junior-powered S.1 were quickly evident.

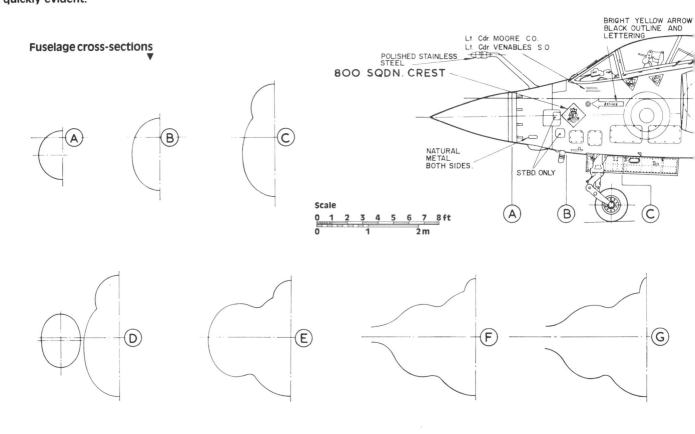

▲
S.2s in flight, the nearest aircraft fitted with 'slipper' tanks. Buccaneers still serve with the RAF and are a very potent force.

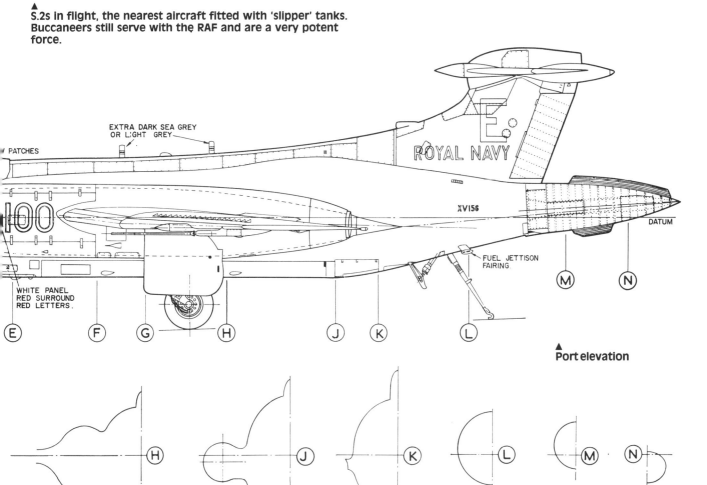

EXTRA DARK SEA GREY OR LIGHT GREY

PATCHES

ROYAL NAVY

XV156

DATUM

FUEL JETTISON FAIRING

WHITE PANEL RED SURROUND RED LETTERS.

E F G H J K L M N

▲
Port elevation

H J K L M N

Colour notes

Prior to December 1966 – Extra Dark Sea Grey top and sides; glossy white under surfaces to datum. Wing serials – Roundel Blue. Fin and fuselage serials and lettering – White. Nose radomes originally natural glassfibre, but later overpainted. Interiors of dive brakes, wing at break, wheels etc – Light grey-green ('duck-egg').

After December 1966 – Extra Dark Sea Grey overall, with pale powder blue serials and fin lettering.

Front elevation
▼

LEADING EDGE
COLOUR BOUNDARY

Scrap views
Underwing stores
▼ ▶

OUTBOARD PYLON

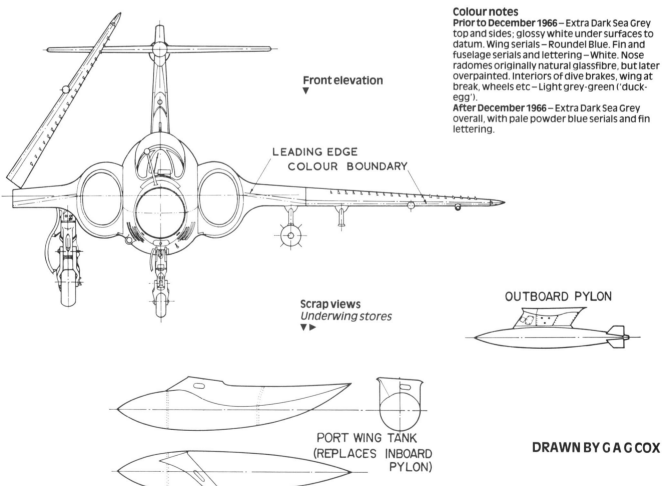

PORT WING TANK
(REPLACES INBOARD
PYLON)

DRAWN BY G A G COX

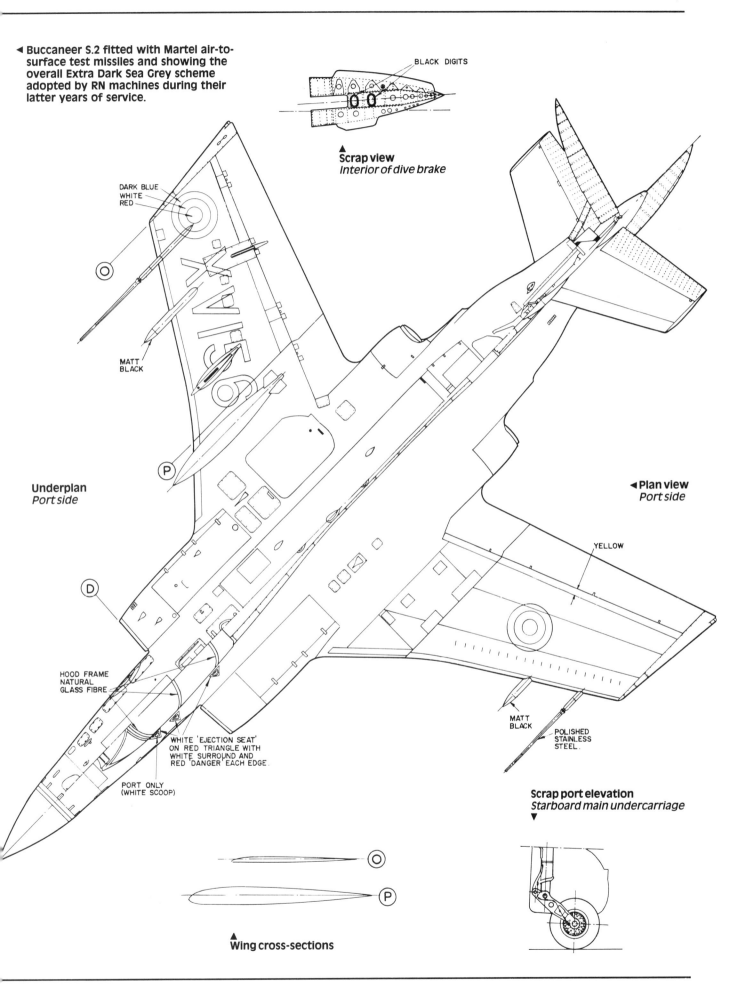

◄ Buccaneer S.2 fitted with Martel air-to-surface test missiles and showing the overall Extra Dark Sea Grey scheme adopted by RN machines during their latter years of service.

BLACK DIGITS

▲ **Scrap view**
Interior of dive brake

DARK BLUE
WHITE
RED

MATT BLACK

Underplan
Port side

◄ **Plan view**
Port side

YELLOW

HOOD FRAME NATURAL GLASS FIBRE

WHITE 'EJECTION SEAT' ON RED TRIANGLE WITH WHITE SURROUND AND RED 'DANGER' EACH EDGE.

PORT ONLY (WHITE SCOOP)

MATT BLACK

POLISHED STAINLESS STEEL.

Scrap port elevation
Starboard main undercarriage
▼

▲ **Wing cross-sections**

Ling-Temco-Vought A-7E Corsair

Country of origin: USA.
Type: Single-seat, carrier-based tactical attack aircraft.
Dimensions: Wing span 38ft 9in *11.81m*; length 46ft 1½in *14.06m*; height 16ft 0in *4.88m*; wing area 375 sq ft *34.84m²*.
Weights: Empty about 18,000lb *8163kg*;

maximum over 42,000lb *19,050kg*.
Powerplant: One Allison TF41-A-1 (Rolls-Royce Spey) turbofan of 15,000lb *6800kg* thrust.
Performance: Maximum speed 698mph *1124kph* at sea level; tactical radius (typical) 700 miles *1120km*; range (ferry)

4100 miles *6600km*.
Armament: One fixed 20mm M61 Vulcan cannon plus up to 20,000lb *9070kg* of external ordnance.
Service: First flight (A-7A) 27 September 1965, (E) 25 November 1968; service entry (E) May 1970.

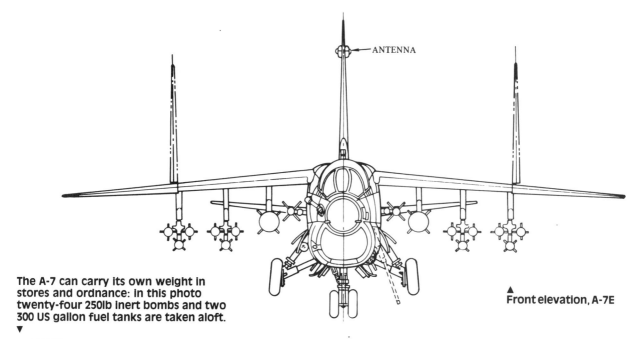

ANTENNA

The A-7 can carry its own weight in stores and ordnance: in this photo twenty-four 250lb inert bombs and two 300 US gallon fuel tanks are taken aloft.
▼

▲
Front elevation, A-7E

▲
Old and new: a WW2 F4U Corsair salutes its modern namesake at LTV's Dallas facility.

Scale

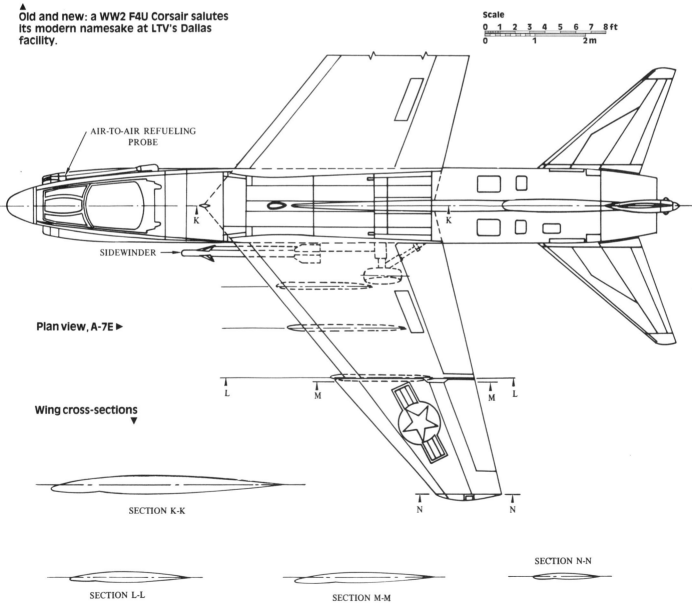

AIR-TO-AIR REFUELING PROBE

SIDEWINDER →

Plan view, A-7E ▶

Wing cross-sections
▼

SECTION K-K

SECTION L-L

SECTION M-M

SECTION N-N

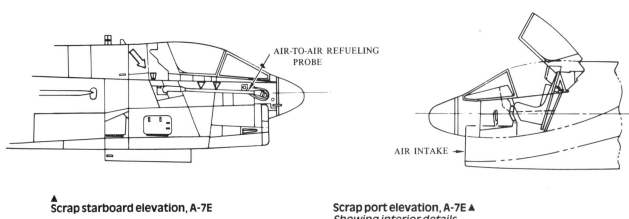

AIR-TO-AIR REFUELING
PROBE

AIR INTAKE

▲
Scrap starboard elevation, A-7E

Scrap port elevation, A-7E ▲
Showing interior details

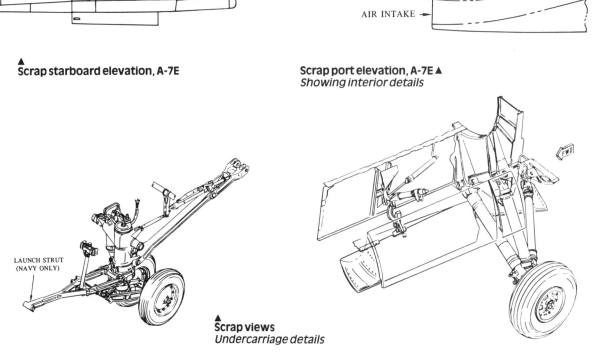

LAUNCH STRUT
(NAVY ONLY)

▲
Scrap views
Undercarriage details

A-7E from VA-195 (USS *Kitty Hawk*), in green and white trim, photographed in 1970.

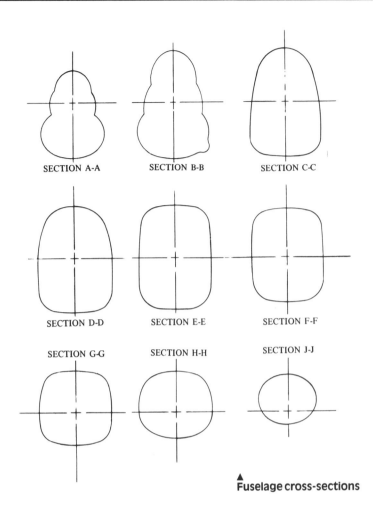

SECTION A-A   SECTION B-B   SECTION C-C

SECTION D-D   SECTION E-E   SECTION F-F

SECTION G-G   SECTION H-H   SECTION J-J

▲ Fuselage cross-sections

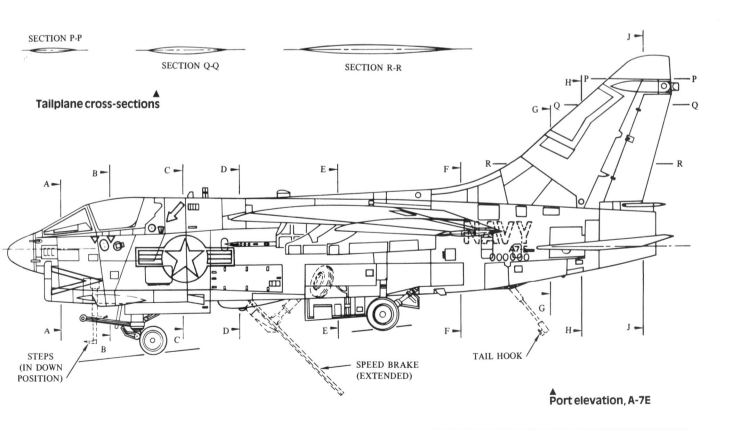

SECTION P-P

SECTION Q-Q

SECTION R-R

▲ Tailplane cross-sections

STEPS
(IN DOWN
POSITION)

SPEED BRAKE
(EXTENDED)

TAIL HOOK

▲ Port elevation, A-7E

▲
The USAF's A-7D is essentially similar to
the A-7E. This 333rd TFTS example has
standard Vietnam-era camouflage.

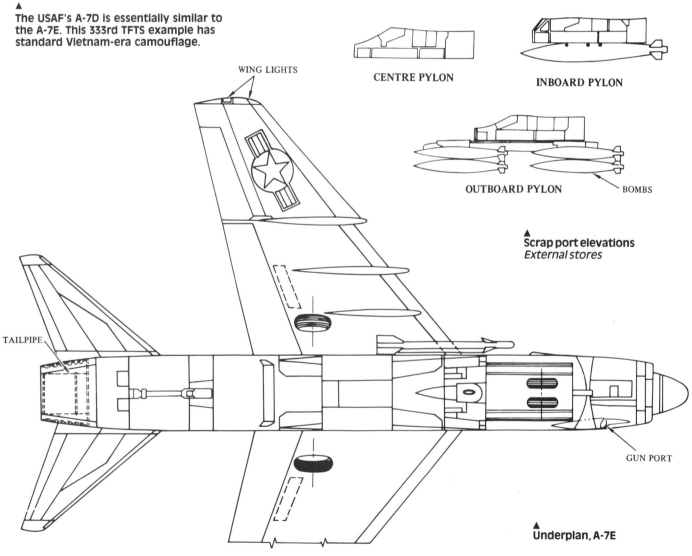

CENTRE PYLON

INBOARD PYLON

OUTBOARD PYLON — BOMBS

▲
Scrap port elevations
External stores

WING LIGHTS

TAILPIPE

GUN PORT

▲
Underplan, A-7E

Rear elevation, A-7E
▼

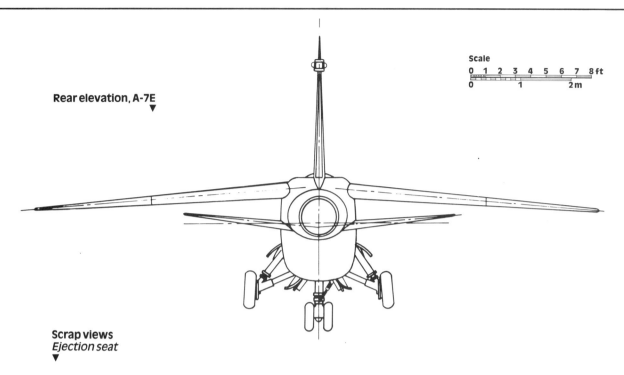

Scale
0 1 2 3 4 5 6 7 8 ft
0 1 2 m

Scrap views
Ejection seat
▼

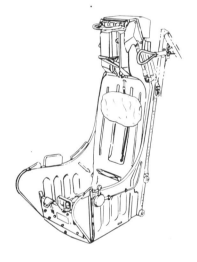

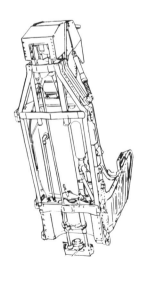

Cockpit layout, A-7E
▼

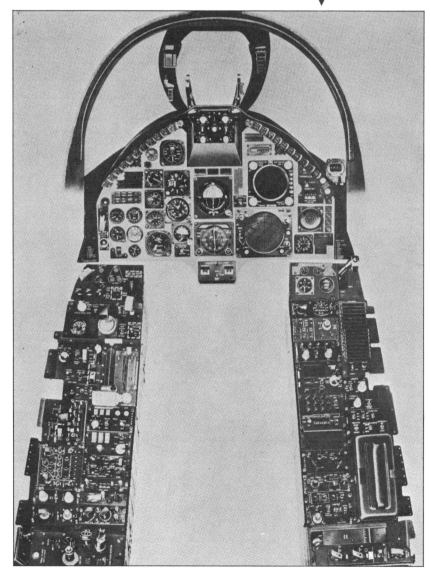

McDonnell F4H-1, F-4K and F-4M Phantom

Country of origin: USA.
Type: Two-seat, carrier- and land-based, all-weather, multi-role fighter.
Dimensions: Wing span 38ft 5in *11.71m*; length 58ft 1in *17.70m*, (F-4K, F-4M) 57ft 7in *17.55m*; height 16ft 3in *4.95m*; wing area 530 sq ft *49.24m²*.
Weights: Empty 27,640lb *12,535kg*, (F-4K, F-4M) 31,000lb *14,060kg*; maximum 54,600lb *24,760kg*, (F-4K, F-4M) 58,000lb

26,300kg.
Powerplant: Two General Electric J79-GE-2 each of 16,150lb *7325kg* thrust, (F-4K, F-4M) Rolls-Royce Spey Mk 202 or 203 each of 20,500lb *9300kg* thrust.
Performance: (F-4K, F-4M) Maximum speed 1386mph *2230kph* (Mach 2.1) at altitude; initial climb rate 32,000ft/min *9750m/min*; service ceiling 60,000ft *18,300m*; range (clean) 1700 miles

2730km, (ferry) 2400 miles *3865km*.
Armament: (F-4K, F-4M) Up to four AIM-7 Sparrow or BAe Sky Flash AAMs plus up to four AIM-9 Sidewinder AAMs, or SUU-23/A gun pod; (strike role) up to 16,000lb *7250kg* of external ordnance.
Service: First flight (F4H-1) 27 May 1958, (F-4K) 27 June 1966, (F-4M) 17 February 1967; service entry (K) 25 April 1968, (M) 23 August 1968.

▲ First of the Phantoms, the subject of the drawings on this page. Note single-place cockpit.

DRAWN BY D H COOKSEY AND C J NICHOLS

Scrap view, F-4A
▼

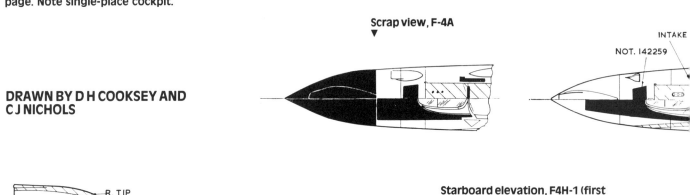

INTAKE

NOT. 142259

Starboard elevation, F4H-1 (first prototype)
▼

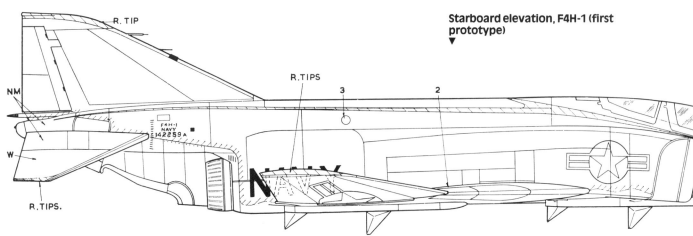

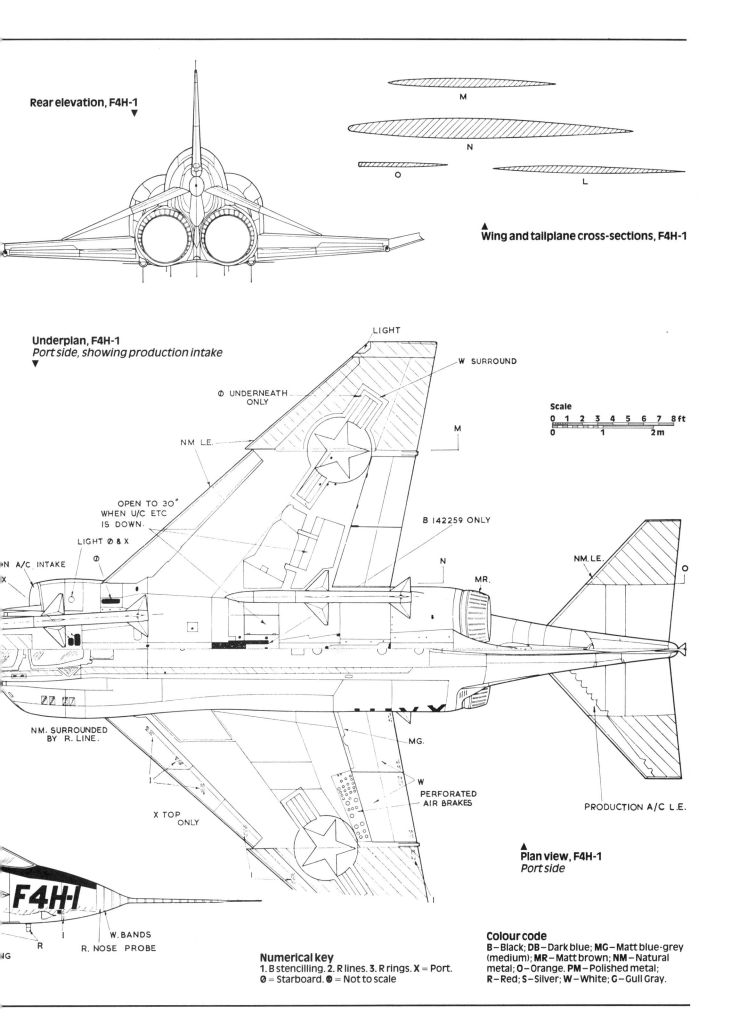

Rear elevation, F4H-1
▼

M

N

O

L

▲
Wing and tailplane cross-sections, F4H-1

Underplan, F4H-1
Port side, showing production intake
▼

LIGHT

Ø UNDERNEATH
ONLY

W SURROUND

NM L.E.

M

OPEN TO 30°
WHEN U/C ETC
IS DOWN.

LIGHT Ø & X

B 142259 ONLY

N A/C INTAKE

Ø

N

MR.

X

NM. L.E.

O

NM. SURROUNDED
BY R. LINE.

MG.

W

PERFORATED
AIR BRAKES

X TOP
ONLY

Scale
0 1 2 3 4 5 6 7 8 ft
0 1 2 m

PRODUCTION A/C L.E.

▲
Plan view, F4H-1
Port side

F4H-I

W. BANDS

R. NOSE PROBE

R

Numerical key
1. B stencilling. 2. R lines. 3. R rings. X = Port.
Ø = Starboard. ⊗ = Not to scale

Colour code
B – Black; DB – Dark blue; MG – Matt blue-grey
(medium); MR – Matt brown; NM – Natural
metal; O – Orange. PM – Polished metal;
R – Red; S – Silver; W – White; G – Gull Gray.

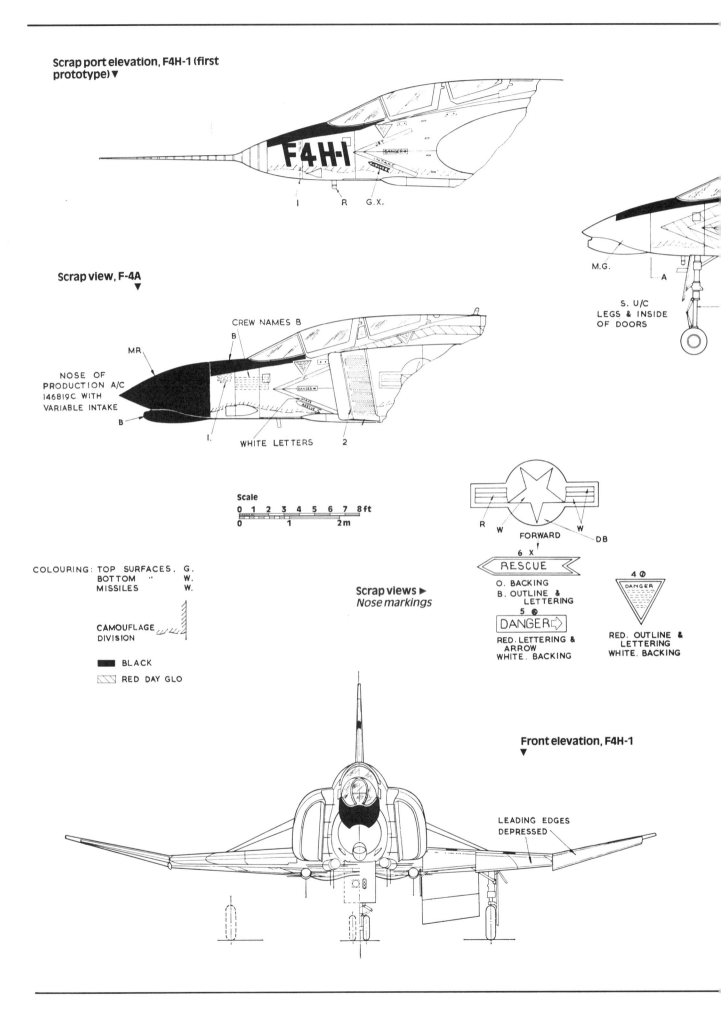

Scrap port elevation, F4H-1 (first prototype) ▼

F4H-1

I   R   G.X.

Scrap view, F-4A
▼

CREW NAMES B

B

MR

NOSE OF
PRODUCTION A/C
146819C WITH
VARIABLE INTAKE

B

I.

WHITE LETTERS

2

M.G.

A

S. U/C
LEGS & INSIDE
OF DOORS

Scale
0 1 2 3 4 5 6 7 8ft
0   1   2m

COLOURING: TOP SURFACES. G.
BOTTOM   "   W.
MISSILES   W.

CAMOUFLAGE
DIVISION

◼◼◼ BLACK
▨▨ RED DAY GLO

Scrap views ►
Nose markings

R   W   FORWARD   W   DB

6 X
RESCUE
O. BACKING
B. OUTLINE &
LETTERING

5
DANGER▷
RED. LETTERING &
ARROW
WHITE. BACKING

4
DANGER
RED. OUTLINE &
LETTERING
WHITE. BACKING

Front elevation, F4H-1
▼

LEADING EDGES
DEPRESSED

Port elevation, F4H-1 (sixth prototype)
▼

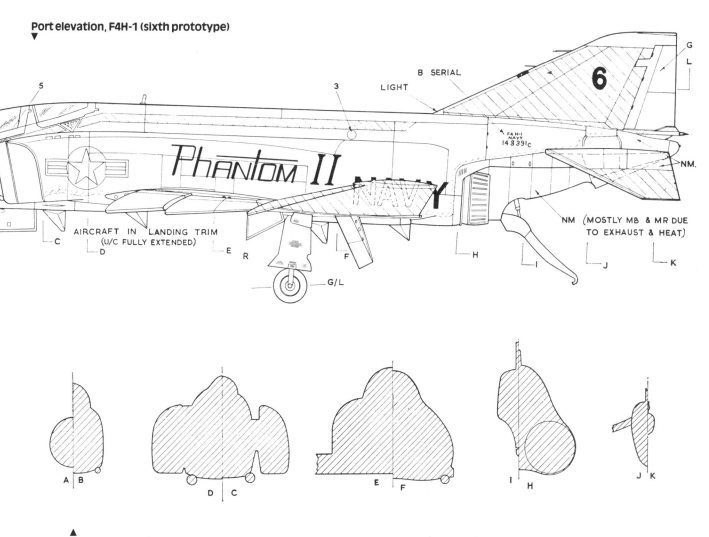

5

B SERIAL

LIGHT

3

6

G

L

F4 H-1
NAVY
143391 C

Phantom II
NAVY

NM.

NM (MOSTLY MB & MR DUE
TO EXHAUST & HEAT)

AIRCRAFT IN LANDING TRIM
(U/C FULLY EXTENDED)

C

D

E   R

F

H

I

J

K

G/L

A | B   D | C   E | F   I | H   J | K

▲
Fuselage cross-sections, F4H-1

**F-4J Phantom variant (nearest camera here, with -N beyond),
from which the Spey-powered F-4K and M were developed.**
▼

Port elevation, F-4K and M
▼

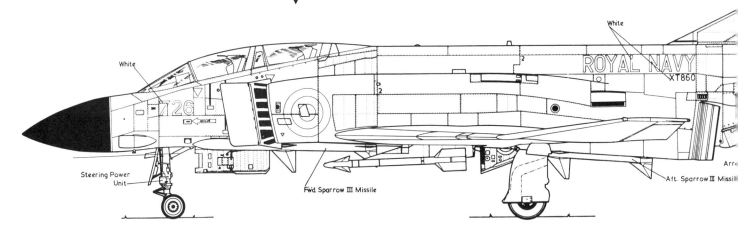

White

White

ROYAL NAVY

XT860

726

Steering Power
Unit

Fwd. Sparrow III Missile

Arre

Aft. Sparrow III Missile

Scrap port elevation, F-4K and M ▼
Showing interior details

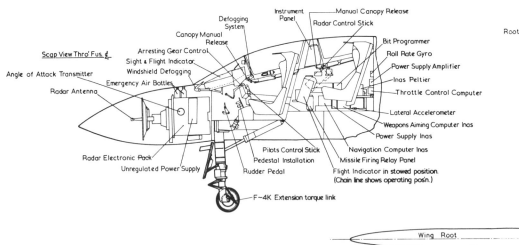

Instrument Panel — Manual Canopy Release
Defogging System — Radar Control Stick
Canopy Manual Release — Bit Programmer
Arresting Gear Control — Roll Rate Gyro
Sight & Flight Indicator — Power Supply Amplifier
Windshield Defogging — Inas Peltier
Emergency Air Bottles — Throttle Control Computer
— Lateral Accelerometer
— Weapons Aiming Computer Inas
— Power Supply Inas
Pilots Control Stick — Navigation Computer Inas
Pedestal Installation — Missile Firing Relay Panel
Rudder Pedal — Flight Indicator in stowed position.
(Chain line shows operating posn.)

Scrap View Thro' Fus. ₵

Angle of Attack Transmitter

Radar Antenna

Radar Electronic Pack
Unregulated Power Supply

F~4K Extension torque link

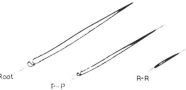

Root

P~P

R-R

▲
**Tailplane cross-sections,
F-4K and M**

Wing Root

J~J

K~K

Wing cross-sections, F-4K and M ▶

725

ROYAL NAVY

VL

◀ **Royal Navy FG Mk 1 (F-4K),
with 'Phantom Phigure'
and RNAS Yeovilton code
letters on tail fin.**

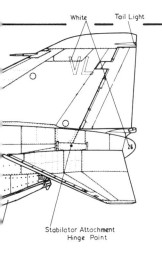

White Tail Light

Stabilator Attachment
Hinge Point

▲
F-4M for the Royal Air Force, generally similar to the F-4K but lacking the slotted stabilisers, catapult hooks and extensible nose-gear strut of the latter.

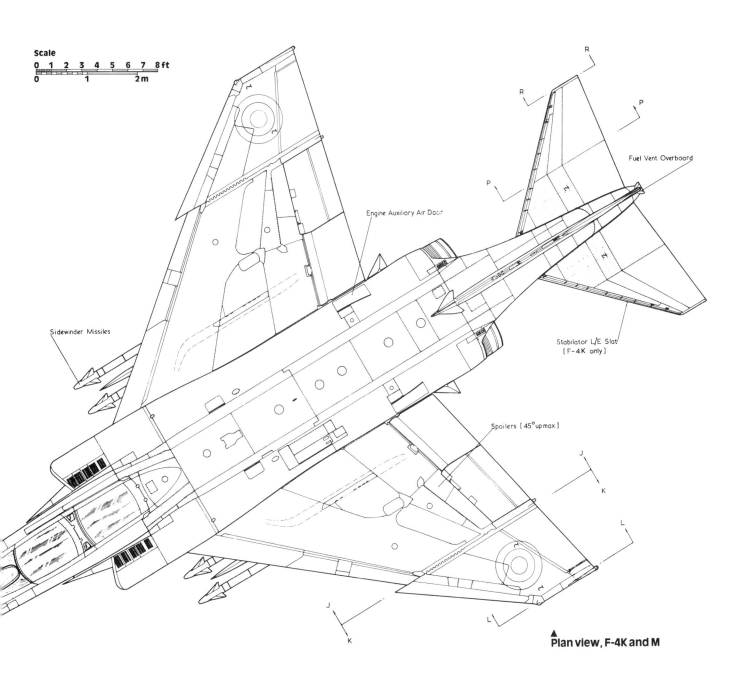

Scale
```
0  1  2  3  4  5  6  7  8 ft
0        1        2 m
```

Engine Auxiliary Air Door

Fuel Vent Overboard

Sidewinder Missiles

Stabilator L/E Slat
[F-4K only]

Spoilers [45°up max.]

▲
Plan view, F-4K and M

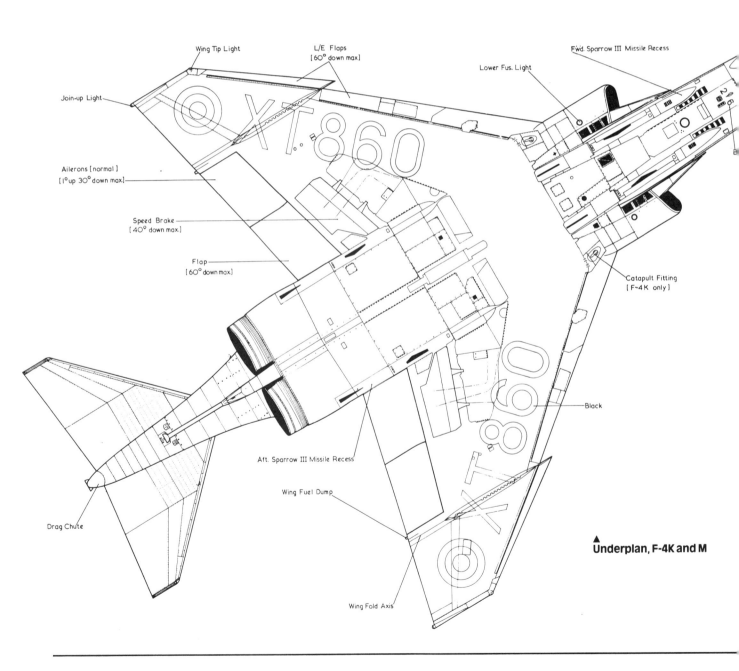

Wing Tip Light

L/E Flaps [60° down max.]

Fwd. Sparrow III Missile Recess

Lower Fus. Light

Join-up Light

Ailerons [normal] [1° up 30° down max.]

Speed Brake [40° down max.]

Flap [60° down max.]

Catapult Fitting [F~4K only]

Black

Aft. Sparrow III Missile Recess

Wing Fuel Dump

Drag Chute

Underplan, F-4K and M

Wing Fold Axis

◄ Re-jigging the Phantom design to accept Spey engines was a complex and expensive process, and the K and M proved to be slower than their US-engined counterparts.

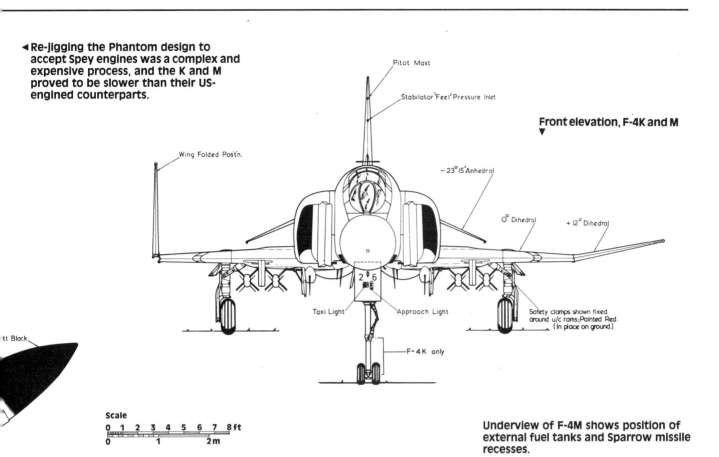

Pitot Mast

Stabilator 'Feel' Pressure Inlet

Front elevation, F-4K and M
▼

Wing Folded Pos'n.

− 23° 15' Anhedral

0° Dihedral

+ 12° Dihedral

tt Black

Taxi Light

Approach Light

Safety clamps shown fixed around u/c rams; Painted Red. (In place on ground.)

F~4K only

Scale

0 1 2 3 4 5 6 7 8 ft

0   1   2 m

Underview of F-4M shows position of external fuel tanks and Sparrow missile recesses.
▼

▲
'Treble-One' Squadron F-4Ms (redesignated FGR Mk 2 in RAF service), with acquisition Sidewinders on inboard pylons.

Wing cross-sections, F-4K and M
▼

L-L

M'

N'

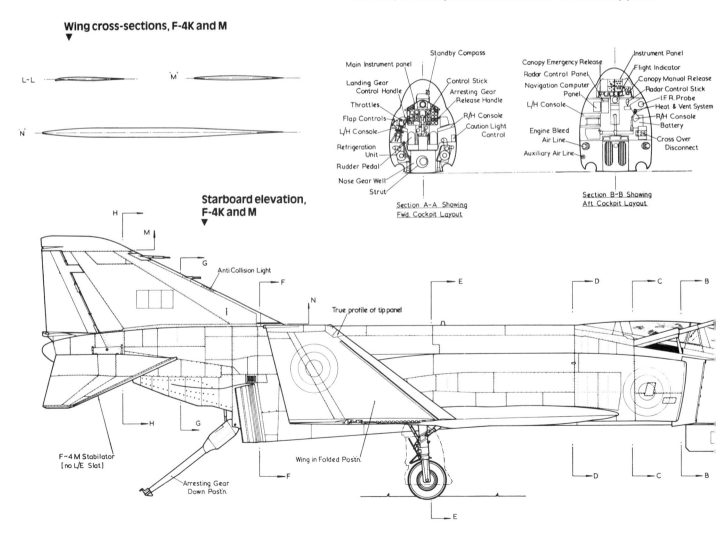

Standby Compass

Main Instrument panel

Landing Gear Control Handle

Control Stick

Arresting Gear Release Handle

Throttles

Flap Controls

L/H Console

R/H Console

Caution Light Control

Refrigeration Unit

Rudder Pedal

Nose Gear Well

Strut

Section A-A Showing Fwd. Cockpit Layout

Canopy Emergency Release

Instrument Panel

Radar Control Panel

Flight Indicator

Navigation Computer Panel

Canopy Manual Release

Radar Control Stick

L/H Console

I.F.R. Probe

Heat & Vent System

R/H Console

Engine Bleed Air Line

Battery

Auxiliary Air Line

Cross Over Disconnect

Section B-B Showing Aft Cockpit Layout

Starboard elevation, F-4K and M
▼

H

M

G

Anti Collision Light

F

E

D

C

B

N

True profile of tip panel

H

G

F-4 M Stabilator [no L/E Slat]

Wing in Folded Pos'tn.

D

C

B

Arresting Gear Down Pos'tn.

F

E

▲
No 111 Squadron again, this aircraft showing its full
complement of (practice) AAMs.

Detail view showing port main gear. Note lash-down lugs.
▼

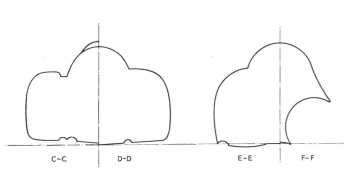

C~C   D~D   E~E   F~F

A

Retractable
In Flight Refueling Probe

Hinged Nose Cone (F~4K)

Communications
Antenna

Radar Dish
Antenna.

Communications
Antenna

F~4M only

dercarriage rams shown
without safety clamps

G~G   H~H

▲
Fuselage cross-sections,
F-4K and M

General Dynamics F-111E

Country of origin: USA.
Type: Two-seat, land-based tactical attack aircraft.
Dimensions: Wing span (maximum sweep) 31ft 11½in *9.74m*, (minimum sweep) 63ft 0in *19.20m*; length 73ft 6in *22.40m*; height 17ft 1½in *5.22m*; wing area (maximum) 525 sq ft *48.77m²*.

Weights: Empty 47,000lb *21,315kg*; loaded 92,500lb *41,950kg*.
Powerplant: Two Pratt & Whitney TF30-9 augmented turbofans each of 19,600lb *8893kg* thrust.
Performance: Maximum speed (clean) 1450mph *2335kph* (Mach 2.2) at 36,000ft *10,950m*; service ceiling 55,000ft *16,760m*;

range (clean) over 3000 miles *4850km*.
Armament: Up to 2000lb *907kg* of bombs in fuselage bay, plus up to 31,500lb *14,285kg* of external ordnance.
Service: First flight (F-111A) 21 December 1964, (F-111E) 20 August 1969; service entry (E) autumn 1969.

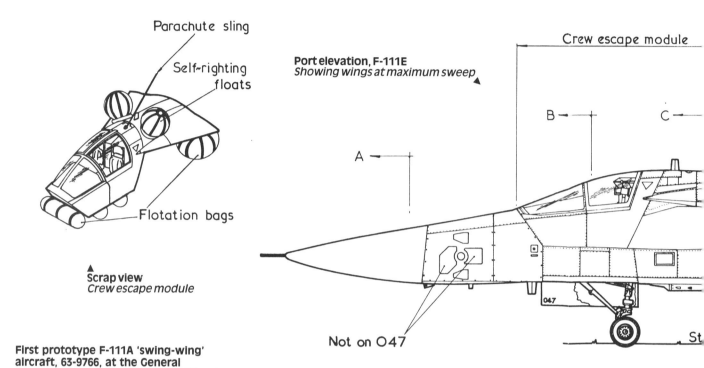

Parachute sling
Self-righting floats
Flotation bags

▲ **Scrap view**
Crew escape module

Port elevation, F-111E
Showing wings at maximum sweep ▲

Crew escape module

Not on O47

First prototype F-111A 'swing-wing' aircraft, 63-9766, at the General Dynamics (formerly Convair) facility at Fort Worth.
▼

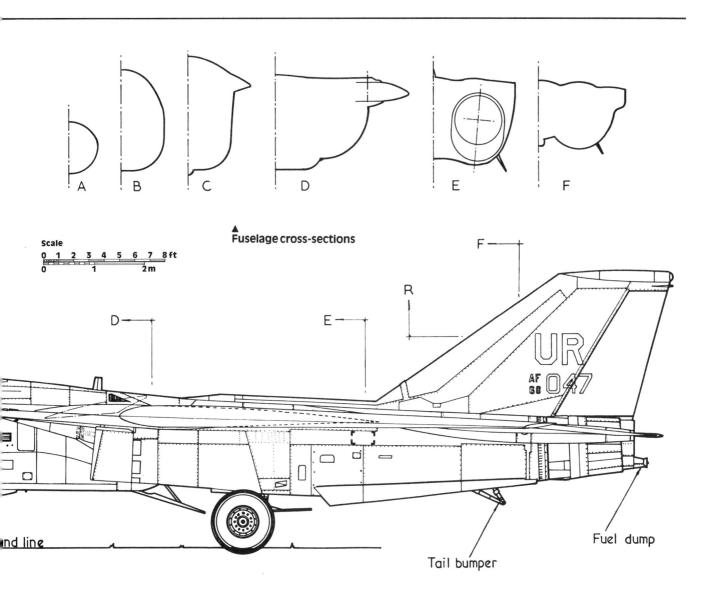

A   B   C   D   E   F

▲ **Fuselage cross-sections**

Scale
0 1 2 3 4 5 6 7 8 ft
0   1   2 m

Fuel dump

Tail bumper

nd line

Tailfin cross-section
▼

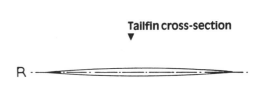

R

◄ **Dramatic low-angle view of 63-9766.**

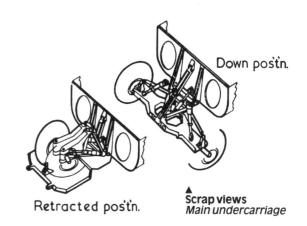

Down pos'tn.

Retracted pos'tn.

▲ **Scrap views**
Main undercarriage

DRAWN BY C J NICHOLS

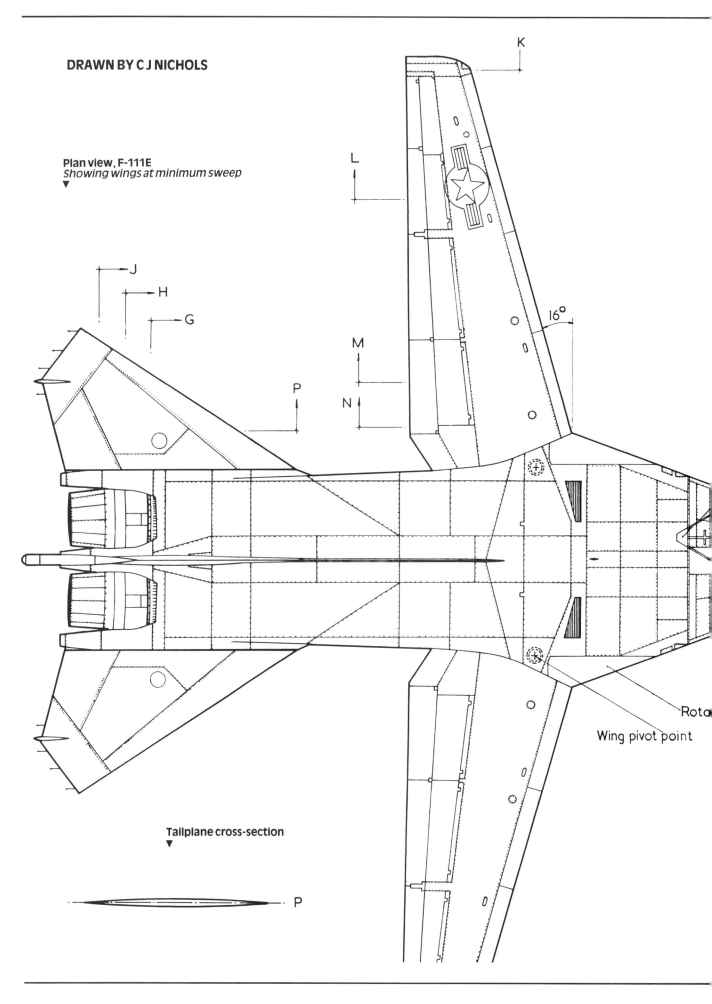

Plan view, F-111E
Showing wings at minimum sweep
▼

16°

Rota

Wing pivot point

Tailplane cross-section
▼

P

▲
After much controversy the Navy's F-111B programme was cancelled, its place taken by the F-14 Tomcat.

ght refuelling

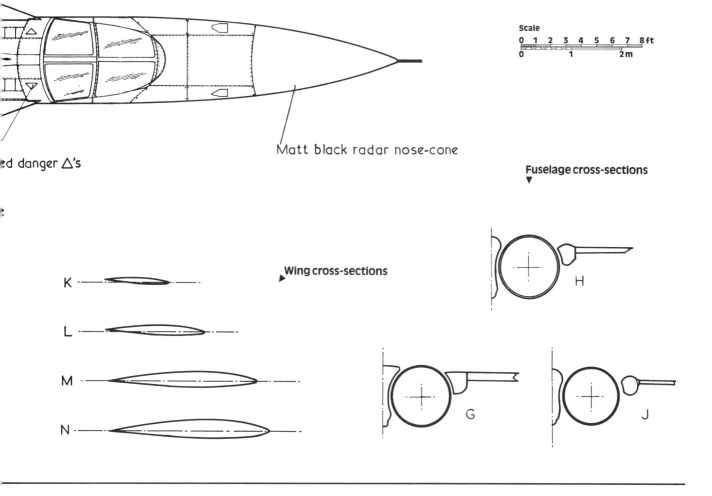

Matt black radar nose-cone

d danger △'s

Scale

0 1 2 3 4 5 6 7 8 ft

0   1   2 m

Fuselage cross-sections
▼

H

▶ **Wing cross-sections**

K

L

M

N

G

J

◄In-flight study of F-111E 68-0054 from Upper Heyford, with yellow fin-tip fairing.

Scale

0 1 2 3 4 5 6 7 8 ft

0   1   2m

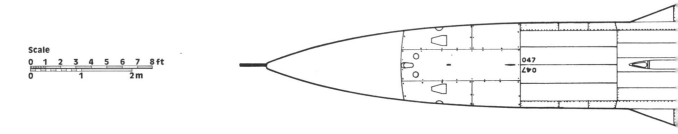

047

Inside the cockpit of an FB-111A bomber. The crew do not have ejection seats – the escape system is the complete cockpit capsule.
▼

Sh◄

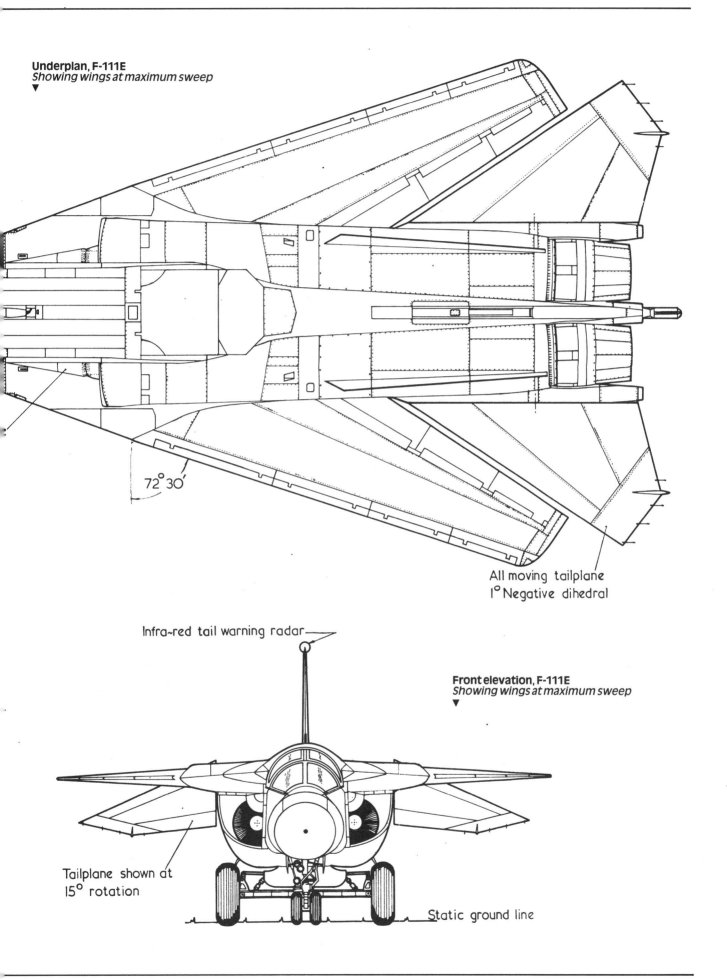

Underplan, F-111E
Showing wings at maximum sweep
▼

72° 30′

All moving tailplane
1° Negative dihedral

Infra-red tail warning radar

Front elevation, F-111E
Showing wings at maximum sweep
▼

Tailplane shown at
15° rotation

Static ground line

British Aerospace Sea Harrier FRS Mk 1

Country of origin: Great Britain.
Type: Single-seat, carrier-based STOVL fighter, reconnaissance and strike aircraft.
Dimensions: Wing span 25ft 3in *7.70m*; length 47ft 7in *14.50m*; height 12ft 2in *3.71m*; wing area 201.1 sq ft *18.68m²*.

Weights: Empty 14,050lb *6372kg*; maximum 26,200lb *11,882kg*.
Powerplant: One Rolls-Royce Pegasus Mk 104 vectored-thrust turbofan of 21,500lb *9750kg*.
Performance: Maximum speed 740mph *1190kph*; maximum intercept radius 400

miles *645km*.
Armament: Two podded 30mm Aden cannon, plus up to 8000lb *3628kg* of external ordnance.
Service: First flight 20 August 1978; service entry 18 June 1979.

Port elevation ▼

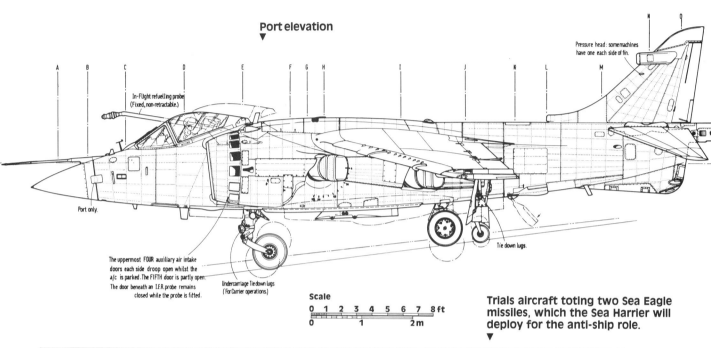

The uppermost FOUR auxiliary air intake doors each side droop open whilst the a/c is parked. The FIFTH door is partly open. The door beneath an I.F.R. probe remains closed while the probe is fitted.

In-Flight refuelling probe (Fixed, non-retractable.)

Port only.

Undercarriage Tie down lugs (For Carrier operations.)

Tie down lugs.

Pressure head: some machines have one each side of fin.

Scale

0 1 2 3 4 5 6 7 8 ft
0   1   2 m

Trials aircraft toting two Sea Eagle missiles, which the Sea Harrier will deploy for the anti-ship role. ▼

▲ 801 NAS Sea Harrier in original EDSG and white scheme prior to the Falklands conflict. Twin Aden gun pods are fitted here.

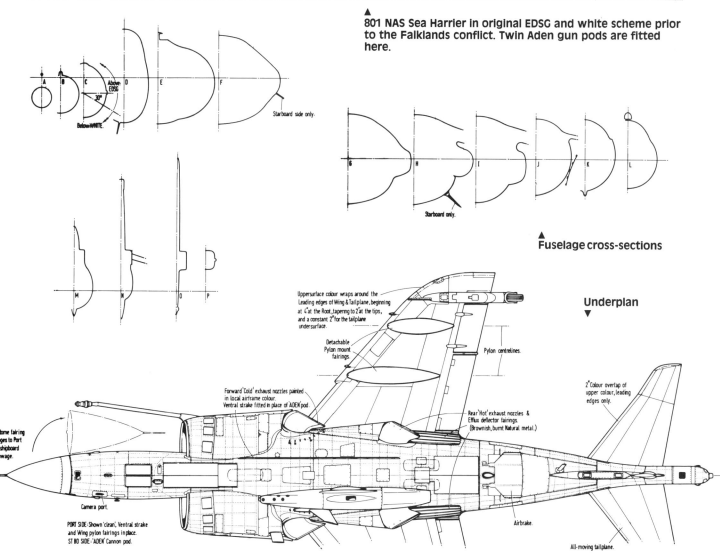

Above EDSG.

30°

Below WHITE.

Starboard side only.

Starboard only.

▲ Fuselage cross-sections

Uppersurface colour wraps around the Leading edges of Wing & Tailplane, beginning at 4" at the Root, tapering to 2" at the tips, and a constant 2" for the tailplane undersurface.

Detachable Pylon mount fairings.

Pylon centrelines.

Underplan
▼

Forward 'Cold' exhaust nozzles painted in local airframe colour. Ventral strake fitted in place of 'ADEN' pod.

Rear 'Hot' exhaust nozzles & Efflux deflector fairings. (Brownish, burnt Natural metal.)

2" Colour overlap of upper colour, leading edges only.

Radome fairing hinges to Port for shipboard stowage.

Camera port.

PORT SIDE: Shown 'clean', Ventral strake and Wing pylon fairings in place. ST BD SIDE: 'ADEN' Cannon pod.

Airbrake.

All-moving tailplane.

◄ Sea Harrier 'office', with radar display (upper right) covered as a security precaution. Nozzle actuating lever is situated on throttle quadrant (left console).

Colour notes

Royal Navy Sea Harriers prior to the 1982 South Atlantic operations were finished in Extra Dark Sea Grey (EDSG) upper surfaces with undersides in white; both these colours were high gloss, the EDSG 'wrapping under' the white by 2in on tailplanes and by 4in–2in along wing leading edge, tapering to tip. Codes, serials, squadron insignia etc were applied in conspicuous colours. At the time of the Task Force's departure the aircraft went aboard *Hermes* and *Invincible* in this scheme, but once heading southwards they had their white under surfaces overpainted in gloss EDSG, obliterating the underwing serials in the process. This 'toning down' included fuel tanks, pylons and missile rails; roundels generally had the white areas overpainted Roundel Blue, and insides of air brakes were now EDSG. A follow-on batch of Sea Harriers was prepared in a new scheme, with the fuselage and vertical surfaces, as well as the upper surfaces of the wings and tailplane (including the 'wrap'), all semi-matt Medium Sea Grey (MSG), with under surfaces in semi-matt Medium Grey (BS4800.18B.21). Interiors of intakes were now semi-matt white, and large amounts of non-essential stencilling on the airframe were painted out.

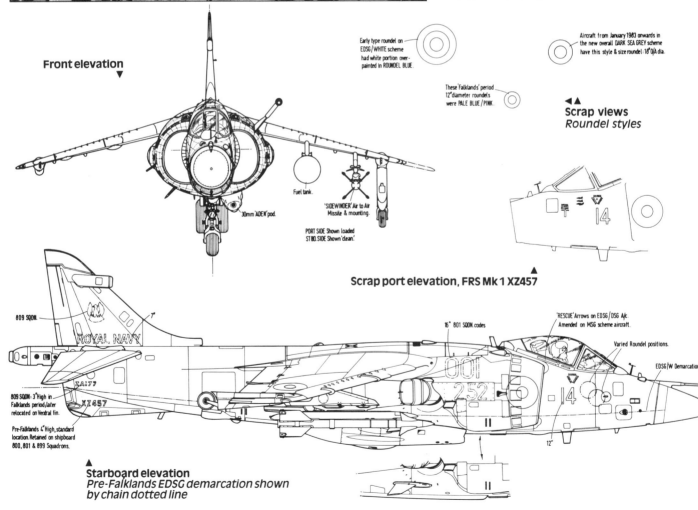

Front elevation
▼

Early type roundel on EDSG/WHITE scheme had white portion over-painted in ROUNDEL BLUE.

Aircraft from January 1983 onwards in the new overall DARK SEA GREY scheme have this style & size roundel: 18"O/A dia.

These 'Falklands' period 12" diameter roundels were PALE BLUE/PINK.

Fuel tank.

30mm 'ADEN' pod.

'SIDEWINDER' Air to Air Missile & mounting.

PORT SIDE Shown loaded
ST BD.SIDE Shown 'clean.'

◄▲
Scrap views
Roundel styles

▲
Scrap port elevation, FRS Mk 1 XZ457

809 SQDN.

ROYAL NAVY

16" 801 SQDN. codes

'RESCUE' Arrows on EDSG/DSG A/c. Amended on MSG scheme aircraft.

Varied Roundel positions.

EDSG/W Demarcation

XA177

XZ457

001
252

14

809 SQDN: 3" High in Falklands period, later relocated on Ventral fin.

Pre-Falklands 4" High, standard location. Retained on shipboard 800, 801 & 899 Squadrons.

12"

▲
Starboard elevation
Pre-Falklands EDSG demarcation shown by chain dotted line

Plan view
▼

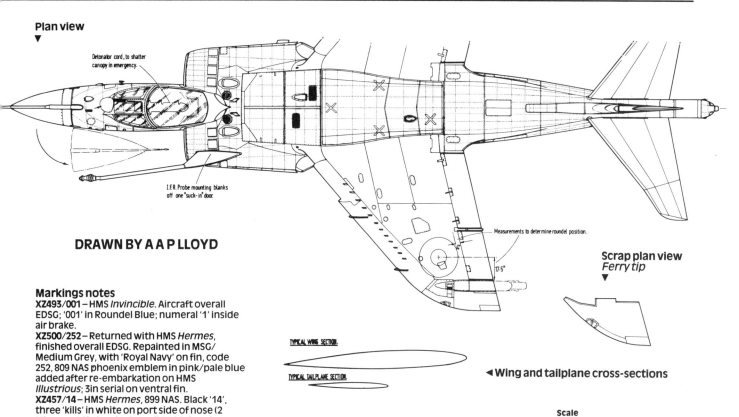

Detonator cord, to shatter canopy in emergency.

I.F.R. Probe mounting blanks off one "suck-in" door.

Measurements to determine roundel position.

17·5"

DRAWN BY A A P LLOYD

Scrap plan view
Ferry tip
▼

Markings notes
XZ493/001 – HMS *Invincible*. Aircraft overall EDSG; '001' in Roundel Blue; numeral '1' inside air brake.
XZ500/252 – Returned with HMS *Hermes*, finished overall EDSG. Repainted in MSG/Medium Grey, with 'Royal Navy' on fin, code 252, 809 NAS phoenix emblem in pink/pale blue added after re-embarkation on HMS *Illustrious*; 3in serial on ventral fin.
XZ457/14 – HMS *Hermes*, 899 NAS. Black '14', three 'kills' in white on port side of nose (2 Mirages, 1 Skyhawk). Overall EDSG (brush-painted undersides); now finished in MSG/MG scheme.

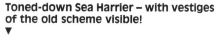

TYPICAL WING SECTION.

TYPICAL TAILPLANE SECTION.

◄ **Wing and tailplane cross-sections**

Scale
0 1 2 3 4 5 6 7 8 ft
0   1   2m

Toned-down Sea Harrier – with vestiges of the old scheme visible!
▼

Scrap elevations
Weapons loads
▼

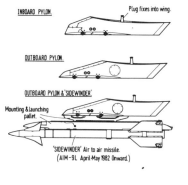

INBOARD PYLON.
Plug fixes into wing.

OUTBOARD PYLON.

OUTBOARD PYLON & 'SIDEWINDER'

Mounting & launching pallet.

'SIDEWINDER' Air to air missile.
(AIM-9L April-May 1982 Onward.)

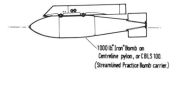

1000 lb. 'Iron' Bomb on Centreline pylon, or CBLS 100.
(Streamlined Practice Bomb carrier.)

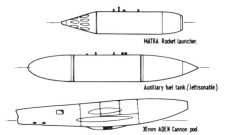

MATRA Rocket launcher.

Auxiliary fuel tank. (Jettisonable.)

30mm ADEN Cannon pod.

British Aerospace EAP

Country of origin: Great Britain.
Type: Single-seat, land-based, technology demonstrator.
Dimensions: Wing span 36ft 7¾in *11.17m*; length 48ft 2¾in *14.70m*; height 18ft 1½in *5.52m*; wing area 559.7 sq ft

52.0m².
Weights: Maximum about 45,000lb *20,500kg*.
Powerplant: Two Turbo-Union RB199 Mk 104D augmented turbofans each of 17,000lb *7710kg* maximum thrust.

Performance: Maximum speed over Mach 2.
Armament: Provision for four Sky Flash AAMs and two ASRAAMs.
Service: First flight 8 August 1986.

DRAWN BY B HYGATE

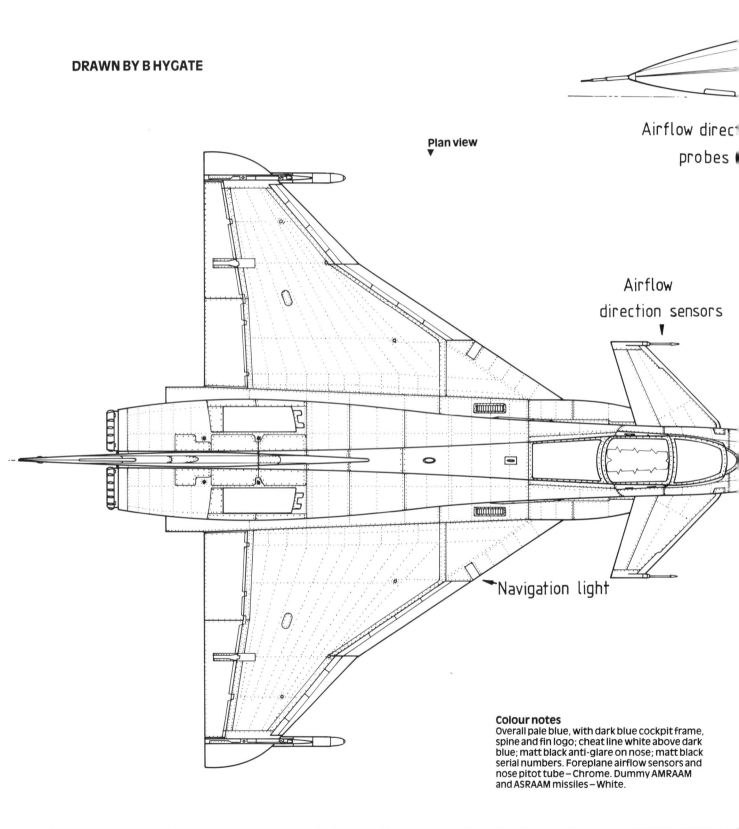

Airflow direct[ion] probes

Airflow direction sensors

Navigation light

Plan view ▼

Colour notes
Overall pale blue, with dark blue cockpit frame, spine and fin logo; cheat line white above dark blue; matt black anti-glare on nose; matt black serial numbers. Foreplane airflow sensors and nose pitot tube – Chrome. Dummy AMRAAM and ASRAAM missiles – White.

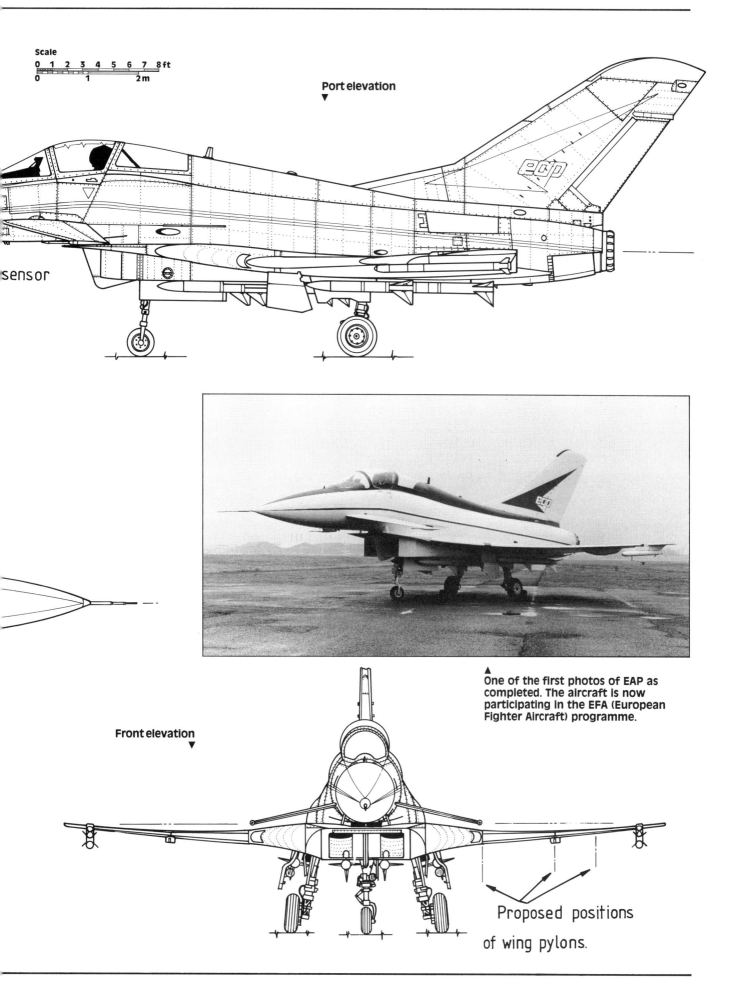

Scale

0 1 2 3 4 5 6 7 8 ft

0 1 2 m

Port elevation
▼

sensor

▲
One of the first photos of EAP as
completed. The aircraft is now
participating in the EFA (European
Fighter Aircraft) programme.

Front elevation
▼

Proposed positions
of wing pylons.

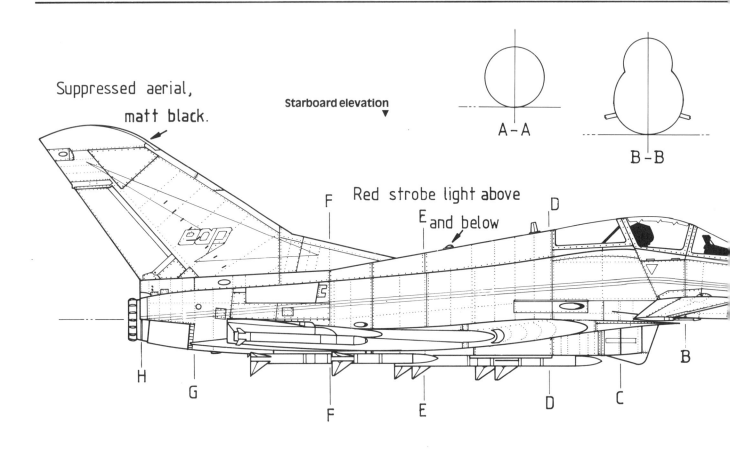

Suppressed aerial, matt black.

Starboard elevation ▼

A – A

B – B

Red strobe light above

E and below

F D

H G F E D C B

ZF 534

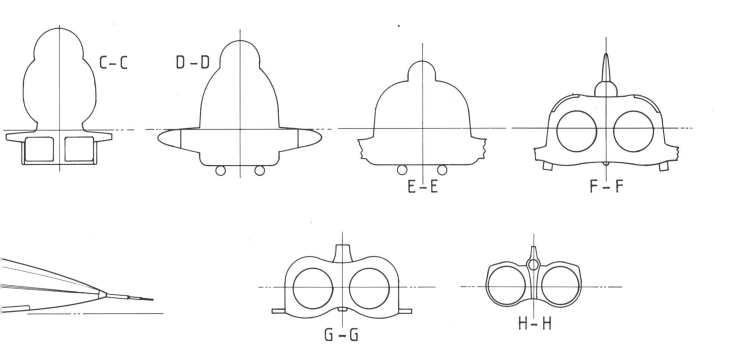

C – C   D – D

E – E   F – F

G – G   H – H

▲
Fuselage cross-sections

First flight, 8 August 1986, during which EAP reached Mach 1.1 and 30,000ft.
▼

EAP's futuristic cockpit display, dominated by a gigantic HUD (head-up display) and with hardly a dial in sight.
▼

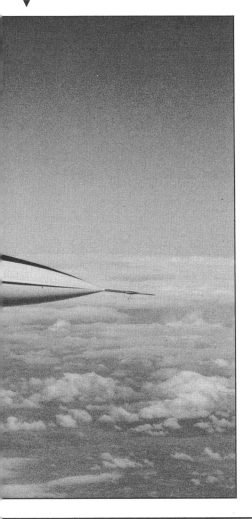

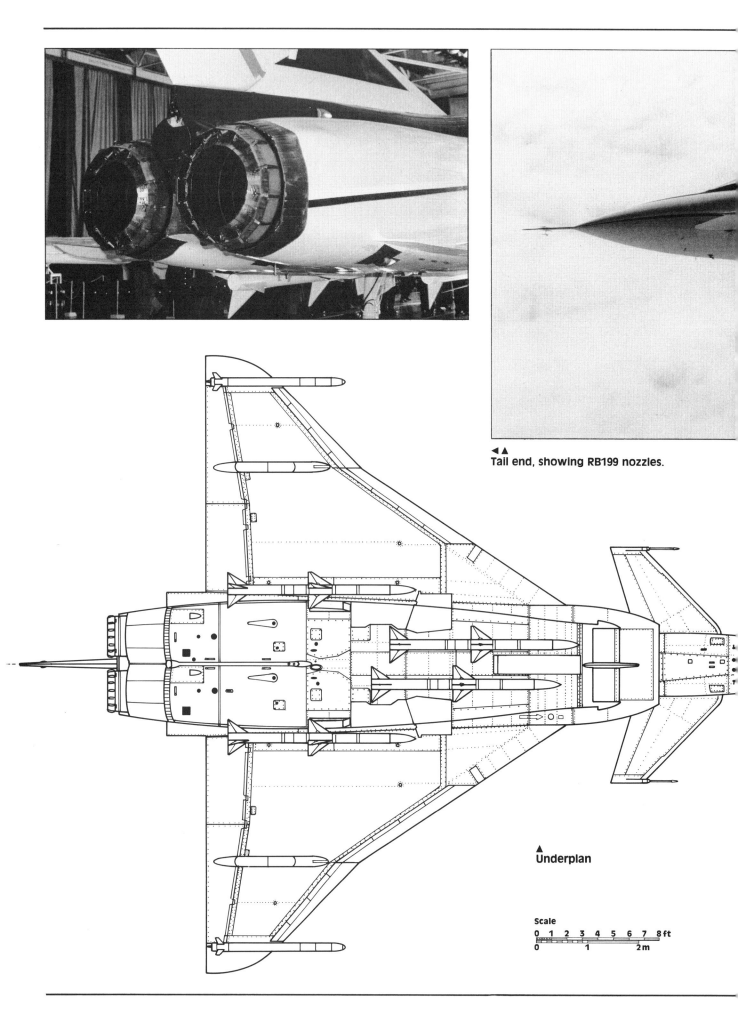

◄▲
Tail end, showing RB199 nozzles.

▲
Underplan

Scale
0 1 2 3 4 5 6 7 8 ft
0 1 2 m

▲
Another first-flight photo, showing to
advantage the (dummy) missile layout.

▲
Ready for take-off, showing the
drooped leading-edge flaps fitted to
the curvaceous wings.

Left afterburner
eyelid shown in
closed position.

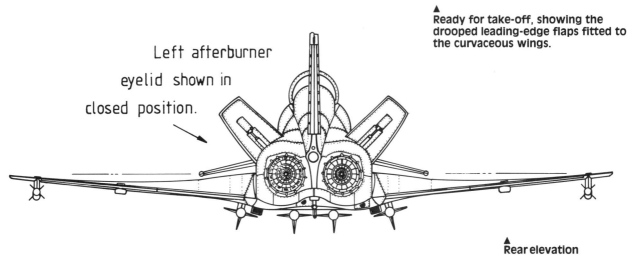

▲
Rear elevation

The Publisher wishes to thank the
following draughtsmen whose drawings
appear in this volume

M A BADROCKE   B HYGATE
GEORGE COX   PAT LLOYD
GEORGE CULL   C J NICHOLS
J R ENOCH   JOHN SILVESTER